Drama Today

Also published by Longman in association with The British Council:

Poetry Today: A Critical Guide to British Poetry 1960–1984
Anthony Thwaite

The Novel Today: A Critical Guide to the British Novel 1970–1989
Allan Massie

Drama Today

A Critical Guide to British Drama 1970–1990

Michelene Wandor

Longman (London and New York)

In association with
The British Council

LONGMAN GROUP UK LIMITED,
Longman House, Burnt Mill,
Harlow, Essex CM20 2JE, England
and Associated Companies throughout the world.

Published in the United States of America
by Longman Publishing, New York

First published 1993

ISBN 0 582 06061 3

British Library Cataloguing-in-Publication Data

A catalogue record for this book is
available from the British Library

Library of Congress Cataloging-in-Publication Data

Wandor, Michelene.
    Drama today : a critical guide to British drama, 1970–1990 /
Michelene Wandor.
        p.   cm.
    Includes bibliographical references and index.
    ISBN 0-582-06061-3 (pbk.)
    1. English drama–20th century–History and criticism.
I. British Council. II. Title.
PR735.W36   1993
822'.91409–dc20   92-46590
                                                                          CIP

Set by 5 in 10/12 pt Bembo
Produced by Longman Singapore Publishers (Pte) Ltd.
Printed in Singapore

Contents

List of illustrations

The Publishers are grateful to the photographer Mark Gerson for permission to reproduce the photographs which appear in this book. Copyright © Mark Gerson, FBIPP.

Preface

Writing a relatively brief guide to British drama produced between 1970 and 1990 has felt at times like an exercise in shorthand. For readers, audiences and many members of the theatrical profession, the extraordinary variety of theatrical entertainment available now appears as a given; the salutary reminder that the abolition of theatre censorship in 1968 revolutionised British theatre seems like a reference to the dark days of history, instead of to a mere quarter of a century ago. And the changes in the theatrical landscape were themselves a part of a wider social and cultural transformation that not only produced new plays, but created a climate in which many of the traditional assumptions about the way theatre was made were challenged.

The structure of this book reflects this, by presenting the context in which the voices of new playwrights came to be heard. The great irony about our modern theatre lies in the fact that the vigour and energy of many of the flagship British playwrights could not have come about without the energy of the – literally – hundreds of small theatres and groups which mushroomed in the late 1960s and early 1970s, who argued about what theatre was for, whom it was for, who it should be by, to whom it should be played, where it should be played, what it should be about and whether its forms should be preserved or challenged. Although some of this process has been written about, and some of the plays published (often after fierce arguments with publishers who felt that only famous playwrights whose work was performed in large theatres were important), the fact remains that it is still the work of playwrights – the texts of the plays themselves – through which our contemporary theatrical history is preserved, and through whom it is taught and disseminated.

I do not in any way want to imply that I value the work of the groups more than that of the playwrights – far from it. One of the great debates of the early 1970s was centred round whether theatre consisted of the performance as text, or the text as literature. The reason that stage plays come to be taught as 'literature' is because they are literary and imaginative texts which lead a double life. On the one hand they are blueprints for the alchemy of live performance, and on the other hand, they survive as a branch of literary study because they have value as fictional texts consisting (almost) entirely of dialogue.

The core of this book's discussion, then, consists of a brief look at selections from the work of some selected playwrights. I have deliberately abstained from the blurb-like practice of listing fifteen playwrights in a single paragraph, with a descriptive phrase for each. This does not seem to me to present any kind of real sense of what these writers are about, and how they develop their arguments, or present the issues which are important to them. And overwhelmingly the drama of the past twenty years has been marked out by its engagement with the present as history, and with the working out of the important issues of the day: changes in world politics, optimism for social change, change within the theatre itself through the voices of cultural groups – women and ethnic writers – who have asserted their need and desire to be part of the cultural landscape. I have aimed, where practical, to look at two plays by each major writer, spanning the twenty years covered by the book. Most are successful, well-known writers, whose work is published and relatively easily available.

This does not necessarily mean that these are the only plays worth reading and staging. My theatre-going over the past two decades has provided some extraordinary evenings, many of plays which will never reach a wide audience, let alone achieve publication, but which have been as well crafted and as exciting as anything in this book. The bibliography at the end of this book demonstrates how much more there is to discover about the British theatre. What you are about to read is only a beginning.

Michelene Wandor, July 1992

1

1970–1990: creativity or crisis?

In *Drama in Britain*, covering the years 1964–73, J. W. Lambert characterized drama as a minority middle-class, middle-aged interest. He saw 'dismay in the experimental theatres' almost total failure to capture, let alone hold, the interest of more than a minute percentage of the rising generations', and despite his acknowledgement of the thousands of amateur dramatic societies, was sceptical about new developments at the end of the 1960s:

> It would be hard to substantiate so far any claim that drama in Britain had acquired much extra resonance from its new-found freedom. . . . Its dramatists are not at the moment at any notable peak of creativity, but . . . compared to the situation thirty-five or even twenty-five years ago, our new plays embody a range of social interest and psychological insight which would then have seemed unthinkable. . . . It docs so . . . to a degree far greater than its minority appeal would seem to justify. What is equally important, its sense of adventure and artistic standards have no less steadily expanded since 1964.

Lambert clearly felt something was stirring, but he could not have foreseen those extraordinary cultural and political changes between 1970 and 1990 which have changed the face of the British theatre in every possible sense: numbers and kinds of venues; a variety of approaches to the making of drama; attitudes to public subsidy; searches for new audiences; enthusiastic playwrights, especially the new cultural voices of women and ethnic writers; realism and politics; above all the agenda (sometimes hidden, sometimes not) which debates the relationship of the individual to his/her society.

By 1973, the last year covered by Lambert's survey, the foundations of this new range of theatrical activity had been well and truly established. The political and cultural conditions which gave rise to this extraordinary flowering of British theatre are outlined in the next chapter. But they could not have come about without the figure of Jenny Lee, Britain's first Minister for the Arts (following the establishment of the Arts Council after the Second World War). Her insistence on the importance of public funding for the arts, on an active campaign to draw new audiences for the arts and to encourage young practitioners, led in the mid-1960s to the building or converting of over 100 theatre venues all over the country. From the mid-1960s to the mid-1970s funding for theatre continued to increase steadily to match the demands of a great variety of new work.

In London, for example, the venues ranged from the large classical companies – the Royal Shakespeare Company, based initially at Stratford-upon-Avon, but later with a London base at the Aldwych Theatre; the National Theatre which finally moved to its custom-built home on the south bank of the River Thames in 1976; and smaller auditoria, which had also become known for fostering the talents of new writers (the Royal Court Theatre in London, Peter Cheeseman's company at Stoke-on-Trent). Gradually jobbing venues began to emerge: two particularly significant theatres were the King's Head, a cramped space at the back of a pub in Islington, North London, where the audience ate by candlelight and then watched a play in the corner afterwards; tales of the cramped conditions (such as sharing the dressing room with the occasional rodent) were legion, but testified to the energy and enthusiasm of all concerned. Verity Bargate, who first worked here, went on to become artistic director of the Soho Poly, a tiny basement theatre behind Broadcasting House, London. This company pursued an unending policy of putting on new plays by new writers, on a shoestring, to a lunchtime audience of about 35 per performance.

This 'fringe' theatre, as it came to be known, soon snowballed. While in 1968 there were perhaps only about half a dozen such theatres in London, by the late 1970s there were over 100. Matching these hastily created permanent venues was a growing number of touring companies, whose working lives consisted of taking set, personnel and show in vans around the country, performing anywhere that could provide an audience – on housing estates, in schools, on university campuses. Many theatres outside London also began to establish Theatre in Education groups (known as TIE), and these groups

2

co-ordinated with drama teachers to provide stimulating theatre on contemporary issues.

The sheer multiplication of theatrical enterprises was caught at its halfway point in 1979, when a *British Alternative Directory* was produced (and for a few years annually after that) to cover the literally hundreds of burgeoning groups and individuals. In 1979 there were 117 companies, 50 companies devoted to education and young people and nearly 100 puppet companies. There were nearly 250 British contemporary playwrights, 140 small regional venues, 47 London venues, plus a directory of 140 arts centres in England, Scotland and Wales.

The pressures on both local and national funding were considerable, because very few of these ventures could be seen as directly commercial enterprises. Initially, levels of funding increased in order to try and meet at least some of the newly emerging needs, but by the second half of the 1970s, the Arts Council sought to rationalize and relocate responsibility for funding. A series of Arts Council reports debated the relative responsibilities of the national funding body, regional arts associations and local authorities. The amount of money earmarked for theatre simply was not enough to cope with the demand. Debates about 'standards' began to emerge: should money just be given to 'the best' and if so, who defined 'the best'? Many people felt that it was wrong that taxpayers' money, paid via the state, should be going to groups of people who were critical of the political status quo; young people should not be paid to bite the hand that fed them, the argument went. Others believed that a healthy and vigorous theatre should reflect all shades of opinion as well as all aesthetic forms, and that those in receipt of subsidy should not be discriminated against on the grounds of their politics.

In 1979, the election of a Conservative government under Britain's first woman Prime Minister, Margaret Thatcher, put the finishing touches to this debate in no uncertain terms. The Conservative Arts Minister, Norman St John Stevas, cut public subsidy to the arts, and thus began a steady erosion of this source of supply. In keeping with their policies on health, education and industry, the Tory policies favoured the privatisation of theatre, directing those expressing need for funds to pursue sponsorship elsewhere. In March 1990 Arts Minister Richard Luce began to implement a plan whereby the Arts

Council (based in London) would finance only the large national companies and other so-called centres of excellence, leaving all other funding to devolve upon the responsibility of regional authorities.

Thus, by the end of the 1980s, there were anxious fears for the continuation of the new theatre. Playwright David Edgar wrote an article in May 1991 in the *Independent*, exactly thirty-five years after the watershed production of John Osborne's *Look Back In Anger* opened in London in 1956. He quoted figures showing that

> from 1970 to 1985 new plays were about 12% of the regional main house repertoire. In the past five years the proportion has dropped to 7%. There has been a shift of writerly energy from theatre to the novel and film. Studio theatres have proved not a staging post but a stopping place, limiting the scope of most new plays to eternal triangles in rectangular rooms. . . . For the first time since 1956 there is a whole generation of talent and young British directors who affect little or no attachment to the production of new work.

A campaign was launched in the summer of 1990 to draw attention to the financial plight facing the theatre. Sir Peter Hall said that the government 'had a conscious policy to dismantle our theatres', and in an article in the *Independent* in October 1989, David Lister wrote that:

> Going to the theatre, concerts and art galleries remains largely the privilege of the well-off and well-educated and of more women than men, research shows. A year-long survey of the habits of 24,000 adults in England, Scotland and Wales has found that people with an annual household income of £20,000 or more have considerably higher levels of attendance than those of lower income groups. Information collected for the Arts Council by the British Market Research Bureau shows that in an average period of four weeks during 1988–89 six per cent of the adult population went to the theatre, four per cent to art galleries, two per cent to classical music and one per cent to jazz.

The outlines of the funding fortunes of theatre between 1970 and 1990 does not mean, however, that enthusiasm for making theatre has in any way diminished. The funding crisis – born, paradoxically, of success – opens up a debate which will always be part of any democratic system in which the arts derive their impetus in part from public subsidy. Many supporters of this subsidy argue that its value lies in more than merely encouraging new work that may not be initially commercial.

As an example of the way the 'seeding' effect of public subsidy worked, the story of Dario Fo's political farce *Accidental Death of an Anarchist* is salutary. In 1973, an actor called Gavin Richards formed a new theatre company called the Belt and Braces Roadshow. Richards had worked with various radical theatre groups and companies, including John McGrath, whose 7:84 company was one of the most lively touring theatre companies of the 1970s (see chapter 4). Belt and Braces was a socialist touring company, which performed plays about topical issues, from a socialist point of view, using music and elements of variety performance to entertain and enhance its message. Their policy was 'to present entertainment which is articulate and socialist – that is to say, created from the viewpoint of working and progressive people who look for a socialist culture'.

Their output mingled the directly didactic with the comic and entertaining, and in 1978 they put on *Accidental Death of an Anarchist*, by the Italian socialist Dario Fo, about police brutality, corruption and helplessness. The play was written in a slapstick *commedia dell'arte* style, and its touring success was such that it then transferred to a West End theatre for a lengthy and immensely successful run. There were those who argued that this constituted a sellout of principles, to be playing radical theatre to the very bourgeois audience whose beliefs it was attacking, but there is no doubt that for the company itself, it was a chance to convey its work to greater numbers of people, as well as providing the company with a degree of financial security. Clearly not every subsidized fringe play will make it to the West End (nor would many of the companies wish to), but the example makes it clear that the interaction between the different categories of theatre is continuous, if unpredictable, and concepts of profit and loss have to be seen against the backdrop of a cultural field as a whole.

In this context, subsidy is a form of investment, in which the yields (income, profit, spin-offs in other earnings) are spread over other fields: tourism for example, encourages people from abroad to come to British theatre. The theatre provides employment and develops new forms which feed into other media – film, television, radio, publishing. It is not a charity, but a form of necessary investment. And that the enthusiasm is there is testified by the fact that despite the apparently desperate funding crisis, in January 1991, the London listings magazine *Time Out* gave its readers a choice of 130 theatres – classical, commercial and 'fringe'.

In order to understand the configurations of the theatrical landscape in this period, beyond the bare bones of its institutional framework, one must understand the outlines of the ideological and political period out of which it developed – the theme of the next chapter.

2

Social and political precedents: post-war affluence and the end of censorship

The 1944 Education Act consolidated opportunities for higher education, and the Labour government of 1945–51 launched a programme of partial nationalization and welfare reform. With the establishment of the welfare state after the Second World War, it was widely assumed that the class war was finally over. By the late 1950s, the impact of the post-war boom was being felt. The expansion of the white collar sector to service material expansion produced a new professional group, and with the increase of consumer goods developed a mass culture distributed through TV, cinema and popular music.

The Campaign for Nuclear Disarmament (CND) and the university-based New Left which both formed during this period, reflected a political concern for more than material improvement. CND, with its concern for a world threatened by the destructive aspects of nuclear power, drew into its membership working and lower middle-class people in a new resurgence of political protest. The New Left initiated a revived interest in Marxist theory and in European Marxist writing, as well as pinpointing the contradiction between the so-called liberal values of an affluent society with education available to all, and the realities of adult life in a society where young intellectual professionals were able to do little more than slot into what they saw as a bureaucratized and technologized capitalism. A melting pot of ideas about the relationship between the economy and individual life generated a literature of socialist thought. This intellectual stimulus in turn provoked discussion about the relationship between politics and art.

At the grass roots level of everyday and personal life, post-war society had a dramatic impact on the family. An extensive rehousing programme eroded the security of many working-class communities and attenuated family networks. New technological consumer affluence brought labour-saving devices for the housewife, vacuum cleaners, fridges, more efficient stoves, all the things that we now take for granted. Matching advertising campaigns emphasized the self-sufficiency of each family unit. One of the effects of this was to isolate the woman at the centre of her individual family. In part this gave rise to a new wave of feminism in British life in the late 1960s.

Through the 1950s and 1960s large groups of people from the Caribbean and from Asia came into the country, beginning to establish the basis of a multicultural society; products of Britain's colonial past now settling into the fabric of British life, and bringing new cultural and religious differences and practices. From this basis, ethnic theatre movements and campaigns for ethnic representation within the theatre arose during the 1970s.

A number of legislative reforms passed by the Labour government during the second half of the 1960s were state responses to some of the changes in personal and sexual life. In 1967 an Abortion Act and an Act partially legalizing male homosexuality were passed. In 1969 the Divorce Reform Act eased conditions for divorce, and in 1970 the Equal Pay Act proposed that equal pay for men and women should become a reality by the end of 1975. The nature of gender roles and individual sexual choice became matters for vigorous public debate and took their place onstage in new dramatic developments.

In tandem with these changes, in 1968 state censorship of theatre was finally abolished. The liberalization of the state's attitude to divorce, certain aspects of sexuality in the family, and the new cultural lifestyles of the younger generation were part of the climate in which theatre struggled for its liberation from censorship, remaining an anomaly among the arts.

Films had to be scrutinized by censors (and still have) in order to be given a certificate to be shown, but only after they were already made. Likewise, books could be prosecuted for being obscene, after publication, but play manuscripts had to be submitted *before production* to the Lord Chamberlain and could not go into rehearsal without his approval. He was empowered to demand changes in the text, and as the influential critic Kenneth Tynan pointed out in the *Observer* in 1965:

Since he is appointed directly by the sovereign, he is not responsible to the House of Commons. He inhabits a limbo aloof from democracy answerable to his own hunches. The rules by which he judges plays are in no way defined in law.

In effect these were unspoken and unwritten laws of censorship. In practice (to quote Tynan again),

> since he is always recruited from the peerage he naturally tends to forbid attacks on institutions like the church and the Crown. He never permits plays about eminent British subjects living or recently dead, no matter how harmless the content and despite the fact that Britain's libel laws are about the strictest on earth. Above all, he feels a paternal need to protect his flock from exposure to words or gestures relating to bodily functions below the navel and above the upper thigh. (*A View of the English Stage*, Paladin, 1975.)

The actual process of submitting plays to the Lord Chamberlain was long and tedious. Once approved, a text could not be changed. Obviously this meant restrictions on subject matter, forms of imaginative expression and the impossibility of very topical plays. Theatre had always found ways round censorship (club theatres between the wars, for instance), but after the abolition of the office of the Lord Chamberlain in 1968 plays could now be about anything, be topical, be subject to change from performance to performance and could include improvization onstage. The end of censorship is critical because it helps explain the fierceness, the intensity and the extraordinary spate of theatrical work which took on religion, the church, royalty. A preoccupation with drama as concerned with both history and the present was given new and strong emphasis. Plays explored topical politics, personal relationships which extended to the exploration of sexual relationships as metaphor as well as in reality, and they used a range of language that was not restricted to what was thought to be socially 'proper'.

Although one should not fetishize the appearance of nudity onstage for its own sake, the end of censorship made possible an emblematic moment in the West End production of the

American hippie musical *Hair*, when, in an event that was curiously both innocent and sensual, the entire cast appeared naked, standing quite still. While the hippie message here was 'peace and love', revealed through the innocence of the naked human body, another perspective on the body politic was revealed through a group-authored play of 1971: Howard Brenton, David Hare, Trevor Griffiths, Brian Clark, Snoo Wilson, Hugh Stoddard and Stephen Poliakoff collaborated in *Lay-By*, based on a case about a wrongful conviction of rape. The play was violent, scatological, ending with two morgue attendants cynically washing the corpses of the three main characters. The sexual violence and the representations of ordinary people, divided into victims and persecutors, heralded the arrival of a new generation of angry young men for whom the freedom to use sexual violence as a metaphor for political disintegration was one essential consequence of the abolition of censorship.

The representation of sexuality, in both a realistic and metaphorical sense, as part of potential subject matter for drama, was finally liberated. The kind of lace curtain repression, so acutely and bitterly caught in Joe Orton's plays of the 1960s, was finally gone, and playwrights were free to treat subject matter in whatever way they chose. Where *Lay-By* was a slickly violent attack on hypocrisy and complacency, Trevor Griffiths' *Occupations* (1970) was an altogether more serious, and more problematic, confluence of political subject matter relying on sexual metaphor. The play is set in Turin, and its foreground plot is a conflict between the Italian socialist leader Gramsci and Kabak, a local trade unionist.

The set is dominated by a bed in which lies Angelica, Kabak's wife, dying of cancer of the womb. She is an aristocrat in whom are symbolized both Kabak's personal emotional crisis, and the decay of the ruling classes. Political disease is represented directly by the image of decay on the site of motherhood. The image is highly emotive, and extraordinarily powerful – but at the paradoxical expense of the representation of the realistic woman. The imaginative success of the image, liberated onto the stage in the service of a history play about the political left, occurs at the very time that in the real social world women were beginning to claim their identity as social beings. In a single play the issues of politics, sexuality, and the representation of women are encapsulated. During the course of the following two decades, these issues were developed in both diverging and converging strands of writing.

It was not simply in theatre that cultural debate was taking place. The lively urban cultural life of the late 1960s, rock music, pop festivals, and the 'underground' culture with its superficially permissive attitudes to pleasure and sexuality, drew on the experiences of the Campaign for Nuclear Disarmament, as well as exploiting the expansion of mass media such as the record industry. As world political events became more momentous (the Chinese cultural revolution in the mid–60s, the American war in Vietnam, the invasion of Czechoslovakia, and the French student/workers protest in 1968), increasing militancy in England from working-class organizations and trade unions, the New Left and students, resulted in a new challenge to perceived class differences. The world seemed to be moving towards socialism.

Then, although there were arguments about whether Soviet or Chinese Communism was the solution to the ills of the capitalist West, at least there was an acknowledgement, a broadly shared unity of opinion, that some form of socialism was held to be the answer to the inequalities and injustices that were evident in the West – the conflict between classes, the conflict between races, the conflict between the sexes. There was a broad front of socialist opinion which brought together many varying strands of radicalism, even while people argued fiercely about the best road to achieve apparently shared aims.

In this respect the 1970s bore certain similarities to the 1930s, when, with the formation of the Popular Front to counteract the threat of fascism, art itself became the site of both creation and struggle. Art was being used to convey a political message, and in the process was being transformed. All kinds of writers, including the new playwrights of the 1970s, who may not consciously have thought of themselves as 'political' were affected by the climate of debate, and this affected their work in a variety of ways.

However, with the election of Margaret Thatcher in 1979 and her decade of rule, two things happened. One was that it was evident that the nation as a whole had not been convinced or inspired by the socialist movement or by the industrial–political struggles that went along with it. And what is perhaps more crucial, the Parliamentary opposition simply did not have the energy or power to defeat the moves towards privatization of industry, welfare, educational services and the arts that the Thatcher government was committed to.

At the same time, the generation of post–1968 playwrights was growing into its middle years; they were settling into relationships, bringing up families, developing their own professional lines of imaginative interest as well as responding to the changing world around them. If they began with a conviction that they could be leaders or supporters, they did not end that way.

By 1990, Solidarity was in power in Poland, Vaclav Havel, a writer, was President of Czechoslovakia, the President of Romania had been shot, the Berlin Wall – that potent symbol of division between East and West – had been demolished. In 1990 Margaret Thatcher resigned. In the Soviet Union, Gorbachev's *glasnost* and *perestroika* led to an internal tension that ended with his overthrow. At the end of the 1960s and in the early 1970s, the dominant urgency was to make sense of the results of twenty years of socialism in the East and of the welfare state in the West, and its relationship to democratic and socialist ideas. By the end of the 1980s, the changes in Eastern Europe, the move from state ownership to, at the very least, a mixed economy and growing receptivity to the idea of private ownership, changed the emphasis and this went along with the further erosion of the welfare state in Britain. Political systems and political ideas remain in flux.

3

New voices, new methods: collaborative theatre and the position of women

Against this broad backdrop, old and new voices made bold and new choices. While playwrights such as Arnold Wesker, John Arden, Tom Stoppard and Edward Bond continued their professional careers, new writers emerged – a younger generation of disaffected young men – Howard Brenton, David Hare, David Edgar – and as feminism and ethnic communities began to flex their creative muscles, women writers – Pam Gems, Caryl Churchill – and writers of West Indian and Asian origin – Mustapha Matura, Farrukh Dhondy – wrote from their experiences to like-minded audiences, placing their own cultures on the theatrical map.

Because this new theatre sought to represent unheard voices, it also questioned received ideas about conventional work processes. In different ways, the alternative theatre sought to democratize the social division of labour in the theatre by developing flexible and collaborative work methods, by introducing theatre to new audiences and by representing the experiences and interests of groups of oppressed and exploited people whose lives and emotions and hopes they felt had not been adequately represented on the mainstream stage.

The alternative theatre raised important questions about the way theatre was organized, produced and distributed: about spaces in which plays could be performed (theatres or not theatres); the audiences to whom they were performed (audiences from different classes and different constituencies of interest); the way in which plays were put together (along traditional hierarchical lines or challenging the division of labour based on hierarchy or on differentiated skills); the subject matter of plays and protagonists through whom the subject matter was played out, whether their class, gender or race or the relationship between private and public life – the 'personal' and the 'political'; the form of plays, for example, explorations of time, or the use of mixed genres.

These new ways of working were, of course, important in
the sense that many radical workers in the theatre industry were
questioning conventional ways of putting on plays. Given that
a piece of theatre can be put together with minimal outlay, it
was logical for people who believed in more collaborative ways
of working to get together and explore new methods. The
history of British theatre in the 1970s is in many ways bound up
with these new theatre companies; from them emerged the new
generation of workers in all skills: writers, directors, technicians,
designers, musicians and performers. With hindsight one can
argue that the 'fringe' process was merely a fortuitously radical
form of apprenticeship, but there is also no doubt that the
debates were passionately felt, and that it was the collaborative
processes of different kinds that effectively 'politicized' many
of the writers who have become the mature playwrights of the
1980s and 1990s.

The idea of collaborative theatre was born in the 1960s,
but took off with great enthusiasm after 1968. One of the
earliest groups, Red Ladder, an enthusiastic group of ex-students
and young political activists, exemplified the 'anyone can do
anything' approach; for quite a number of years the group's
members all did a bit of everything – writing, performing,
administration. In the early years the group created plays
about immediate topical issues – housing, trade unions, equal
pay – touring and performing to working-class audiences,
following each performance with discussions and political
consciousness-raising.

By the mid 1970s groups were proliferating rapidly, among
them the Joint Stock theatre company, founded in 1975 by an
all-male group consisting of William Gaskill, former artistic
director of the Royal Court Theatre, Max Stafford-Clark, later
to become artistic director of the same theatre, David Aukin
and David Hare. Their first play was Hare's adaptation of the
documentary book *Fanshen* by William Hinton, which described
the process of transition to Communism in China. Hare was
already established as an eloquent, biting satirical playwright,
but here he was engaged in a work process very different
from the isolated methods of the freelance playwright. It was a
fascinating case of the process which was being dramatized and
reflected in the methods of the creators. The group researched,
discussed, made joint decisions; in rehearsals they discussed the

political point of scenes and characters' motivations, as opposed to the more conventional approach of individual motivation and emotional dynamic.

Joint Stock's links with the Royal Court meant that their work had a far higher profile and greater financial security than many other companies; it also helped provide a political proving ground for a number of writers, including Caryl Churchill, whose play about the English Revolution in the 17th century, *Light Shining in Buckinghamshire*, was created in 1976. Churchill, also already an established radio and stage playwright, had earlier in the same year written *Vinegar Tom*, a play about witchcraft in the 17th century. This play was commissioned by another young company, Monstrous Regiment, consisting of a majority of women with a radical commitment to improving the position of women in theatre. The founding of this company was preceded by the more prosaically named Women's Theatre Group, which grew out of street agitprop performances by women on demonstrations and at conferences in the opening years of the 1970s. Their group was all-female, and their plays were entirely woman-centred; based on subject matter chosen for its 'issue' value: plays about teenage sexuality, inter-generational relationships, female solidarity, women at work. Much of their early work was aimed at schools and young people, and, unlike the theatre-based Joint Stock, they followed performances with discussions on the position of women.

Interestingly, although these and other groups set store by some form of collaborative process, the emergent plays had clear single authorship. Inevitably this makes the matter of authorship appear conventional, when the process and the input often was not, and is in danger of obscuring the interdependence of writers and other workers which was so formative in developing the social perceptions of the writers who subsequently became the well-known playwrights of the 1980s.

The work of women's theatre companies began the process of scrutiny and action on behalf of the position of women in theatre. Any survey of the credits of British plays at the end of the 1960s would have revealed a dominance of men in every sphere. By 1983, a directory of playwrights contained 547 writers, of whom only about one fifth were women. This is in itself not a very high percentage, when one remembers that anyone who wanted to be listed could appear. In *Contemporary Dramatists* (St James's Press, 1977) women represented just under ten per cent of a selected 321. By contrast, the plays published by Samuel French for amateur performance reveal that women writers are in the majority when it comes to writing plays for all-female casts, and this also forms the largest category of plays for the amateur market, reflecting the fact that more women than men are active in amateur dramatic societies.

However, despite these small changes, the catalogue of Britain's largest drama publishers, Methuen, revealed a character count in 1985 for their published plays; these contemporary plays divide roughly into a ratio of two and a half male characters to each female character. We can see from this that we are still very far from a position of male-female parity, whether in the theatrical workforce or in the balance of emphasis in the content of plays.

The position of women in the theatre is in many ways similar to the position they hold in other areas of work. Clustered around the base of the labour pyramid in terms of earnings and artistic and administrative power, very few women reach the top, and in a profession dogged by high unemployment actresses fare worse than actors. Their average earnings are lower and most acting companies support twice as many men as women. On the production and administrative side, women dominate the traditional servicing fields: secretarial, clerical and publicity. On the artistic side the prime creative positions of writer, director and artistic director are still largely held by men. And whereas women have played a central part in the tradition of writing novels, writing for the theatre has not been something that they have chosen easily. On the technical side of theatre work, women are in an even smaller minority. Prejudice against women working in technology, and a hesitancy on the part of women themselves, has ensured that it remains a male-dominated area.

This lack of sexual equality in the theatre has consequences in the subject matter of drama. It has meant that most plays written this century embody the male outlook, and express a view and counter-view very much within a system of aesthetic thinking in which the male is the norm, and in which the central protagonist(s) is (are) invariably male. Women, when they do figure, are either adjuncts to those male protagonists or are seen as ciphers for male concerns. Women have rarely been the subjects of drama either in their own right or in relations with men.

The situation has not arisen as a result of a massive and conscious conspiracy among men, but rather as an often unconscious consequence of the accepted norms of relations between the sexes in society. This is based on an ideology which assumes that biological differences between men and women must necessarily mean that their fields of social activity are different and that men's work is more significant than women's work, which can in turn fuel the argument that women are simply not capable of taking power in the theatre.

Of course it is possible for anyone to quote a number of exceptions – women writers whose work is known and performed all over the world, women directors who have achieved acclaim and produced exciting theatre work, the occasional woman who works as the artistic director of a theatre. The point is not that individual women can't break through; they can, and will continue to do so. But they still remain the exceptions who prove the rule.

4

Language and politics: the senior generation – Stoppard, Pinter, Bond, McGrath

The changes described earlier were, of course, part of a continuum. Playwrights such as Tom Stoppard, Edward Bond, Harold Pinter and Ann Jellicoe continued working in the new climate. Stoppard, in particular, continued a long and successful career begun in 1960. Stoppard has always seen himself as someone who enjoys playing with ideas, rather than embracing open polemics. In his hugely enjoyable comedy, *Rosencrantz and Guildenstern are Dead* (1972), taking two minor characters from Shakespeare's *Hamlet*, he weaves a teasing question about the interplay of illusion, reality and perception itself. He takes the basic precepts of socialist thinking – dialectical materialism – and turns them on their heads. He plays also with current preoccupations of audience-performer relations by placing two characters (theatre critics) in the audience, in a coup of comic theatrical invention.

This pattern continues through the following two decades. Stoppard hooks into exactly the same concerns as his younger contemporaries, but treats them all with his particular brand of intellectual gymnastics, wit and, ultimately apolitical verve. Two works, *Travesties* (1974) and *Hapgood* (1988) exemplify these shifting concerns: the first explores the relationship between art and political commitment, the second the nature of national identity and the crisis in relations in the socialist countries. The main characters in *Travesties* are Lenin, James Joyce, the Dadaist artist Tristan Tzara, and the more obscure figure of Henry Carr, who is derived from a footnote to Joyce's novel, *Ulysses*.

The play is set in Zurich, in Henry Carr's flat, and in a section of the Zurich public library: 'Most of the action takes place within Carr's memory which goes back to the period of the First World War.' The opening shows Tzara putting together a poem made out of random word association. Meanwhile, James Joyce writes sections of *Ulysses*, dictating them to Gwen, Carr's sister. Both wordsmiths sound as though they are talking nonsense, although they appear to understand one another.

After dialogue in Russian between Lenin and his wife Nadia, the play moves into a long monologue, full of good-humoured sophisticated nursery wit, as Carr talks about working for the consular service, and about being cast by Joyce in 'that quintessential English jewel *The Importance of Being Earnest*'.

Isolated in the limbo of Switzerland where there is no war, the play jousts with time. Stoppard: 'The scene . . . is under the erratic control of old Carr's memory . . . One result is that the story (like a toy train perhaps) occasionally jumps the rails and has to be restarted at the point where it goes wild.' The Russian Revolution is reported to Carr, who doesn't understand what has happened. He thinks it involves 'unaccompanied women smoking at the opera, that sort of thing'. When enlightened that it is a revolution between classes, he doesn't take that a lot more seriously, assuming it is something to do with the servant problem.

Tzara and Joyce visit Carr. There is a surreal conversation between them in rhyme. Carr has contempt for artists: 'My dear Tristan, to be an artist at all is like living in Switzerland during a world war.' Tristan claims to be in love with Gwen, who gets muddled up in their imaginations with Gwendoline from Wilde's play, while Tzara gets confused with the character Jack. Characters from reality, history and fiction intermingle in a world entirely set in the imagination.

Act II begins with a long lecture from Cecily, the librarian, about Marx, and the Russian translation of his theoretical work, *Das Kapital*, in 1872, about social theories, terrorism and the proletarian revolution. Cecily defends a material understanding of the nature of art: 'We live in an age when the social order is seen to be the work of material forces and we have been given an entirely new kind of responsibility, the responsibility of changing society.' Carr responds: 'My dear girl – art doesn't change society, it is merely changed by it.' Cecily: 'Art is society, it is one part of many parts, all touching each other, everything from poetry to politics.' Carr argues that Marx got it wrong, and Cecily accuses Carr of arguing politics with her while trying to imagine her naked.

Tom Stoppard

At this point Lenin's wife, Nadia, enters and addresses the audience about Lenin and his belief in state control of literature, against what he called, in 1905, 'bourgeois anarchist individualism'. At the same time, Nadia tells us that he was moved to tears when he saw Alexandre Dumas's *La Dame Au Camelias* in London in 1907. Serious speeches on revolutionary ideas about art and politics are followed by witty rhyming dialogues between Cecily and Gwen having tea in a send-up of English musical comedy styles.

The play ends with a sentimental reminiscence:

> Great days during the war, refugees, spies, exiles, painters, poets, radicals, writers of all kinds, I knew them all. Used to argue far into the night . . . I learned three things in Zurich during the war. I wrote them down. Firstly, you're either a revolutionary or you're not, and if you're not you might as well be an artist as anything else. Secondly, if you can't be an artist you might as well be a revolutionary . . . I forget the third thing.

Stoppard draws together a number of contemporary cultural preoccupations, particularly those that were being acted out within the theatre itself. At the same time, he constantly undermines the ideas by showing the charm of English traditions of metropolitan literary entertainment. The play, stylistically influenced by Dadaism, is a satire on English culture. It is about language, a celebration of a particular kind of literary upper-class wit, in which art is the subject of debate. While Europe is engaged in serious revolutionary wars, the English are preoccupied with the minutiae of literary jokes, propriety and amateur dramatics. The play implies that people create their own myths, that history in its way is a kind of fictional myth and political change mere grist to the fiction writer's mill.

Hapgood is set in the men's changing room of an old-fashioned municipal swimming baths. In the opening scene, Hapgood, a female secret agent whom everyone calls 'Mother', encounters another agent. There is much play with radio receivers, and the panoply of spying. A debate ensues about objective reality and science: 'A double agent is more like a trick of the light. Look, look at the shadow. It is straight like the edge of the wall that makes it. Your Isaac Newton saw this and he concluded that light was made of little particles.' A discourse on the nature of physics and light particles follows, concluding 'that the act of observing determines the reality.' A parallel is drawn in terms of spying:

> I meet my Russian friend Georgi and we exchange material. When the experiment is over, you have a result. I am a British Joe with a Russian source. But they also have a result, because I have given Georgi enough information to keep him credible as a KGB control who is running me as a sleeper. That is what he thinks he is.

A pair of twins further demonstrates the hypothesis that reality is as elusive as fiction, and Kerner, a Russian (who may be the father of Hapgood's son) says he prefers physics and science to art:

> I don't understand this mania for surprises. If the author knows, it's rude not to tell. In science it is understood what is interesting is to know what is happening. When I write an experiment, I do not wish you to be *surprised*, it is not a *joke*. That is why a science paper is a beautiful thing. First here is what we will find, now here is how we find it. Here is the first puzzle, here is the answer. Now we can move on. This is polite. We don't save up all the puzzles to make a triumph for the author – that is the dictatorship of the intelligentsia.

At the end of the play, this view is extrapolated to apply to East-West comparisons:

> The West is morally superior in my opinion. It is in different degrees unjust and corrupt like the East, its moral superiority lies in the fact that the system contains the possibility of its own reversal – I am enthralled by the voting. To me it has power of an equation in nature, the masses converted to energy. Highly theoretical of course, but it means the responsibility is everybody's. You cannot pass the blame to a few gangsters. I prefer that, but I don't need to live with my preference.

Stoppard's view that Western democracy is the more dialectical, is also the cornerstone of his dramatic method; now you see it, now you don't. Every statement can be contradicted, every established stage reality reversed, and all with the power of the spoken word.

Like Tom Stoppard, Harold Pinter is a careful and consummate stylist; but whereas Stoppard cultivates urbane, elaborate intellectual wit, Pinter's reputation has been based on spare, elliptical, allusive dialogue. His halting half-statements, his portrayal of the vulnerability of the individual in the face of often unidentifiable sinister forces. The trend continued into the 1970s, with *No Man's Land* (1975).

This play is set in a house in north-west London. Two men, Hirst and Spooner, have met on Hampstead Heath. Spooner is a lonely poet, interested in the world of the imagination, not experience: 'I have never been loved. From this I derive my strength.' He avoids feeling: 'My own security . . . rests in the confirmation that I elicit from people of all kinds a common and constant level of indifference. It assures me that I am as I think myself to be, that I am fixed, concrete.' There are hints in this conversation that perhaps the two men are one and the same person. Hirst comments: 'No man's land . . . does not move . . . change . . . or grow old . . . remains . . . for ever . . . icy . . . silent.'

Two other men arrive, Foster and Briggs: their conversation is altogether much cruder, men among men travelling the world. They appear to be Hirst's guardians, of his wealth, of his class, who are also, in some form, his jailers. As they say: 'It's a world of eighteenth century cookery books, it's nothing to do with toffee apples and a packet of crisps . . . It's organisation.' It is a world of class differences; it is also a world in which men serve other men. Men with sex and experience serve men who simply sit in the midst of their wealth.

In Act II Briggs brings breakfast: dishes covered by silver lids and a bottle of champagne. Spooner has been locked in a room overnight, and now he has to go to a poetry meeting at a pub in Chalk Farm. Hirst enters, treating Spooner as a colleague with whom he was at Oxford and with whose wife he had an affair. Their exchanges are cocktail party chit-chat about old acquaintances. Spooner accuses Hirst of being a rake. Briggs then refuses to obey Hirst's order to pass the bottle of

Harold Pinter

champagne. Spooner finally does so. Spooner appeals to Hirst to take him on as his secretary. And at the end Spooner repeats: 'You are in no man's land which never moves, which never changes, which never grows older, but which remains forever icy and silent.' Hirst says: 'I'll drink to that.'

Hirst is an established writer. The play alludes to the self-imposed isolation of the writer, hemmed in and protected by figures who protect him but who are also his enemies. The class relations between the two pairs of men are presented as fixed and immutable, symbiotically locked together.

One For The Road was produced during 1984, in America, Holland, Japan, Hungary, Canada, New Zealand, Australia and South Africa. Prevailing critical assumption until this point had been that Pinter's plays were 'absurd', concerned with abstractions and the minutiae of communication between individuals. However, Pinter himself began to contradict this, claiming in the 1980s that his consciousness had always had a political edge to it:

In 1948 I was a conscientious objector, that was a political act. I was terribly disturbed as a young man by the Cold War and McCarthyism. I smelt that American thing a mile off actually and it was very strong . . . In 1948 the Russian suppression of Eastern Europe was an obvious and brutal fact, but I felt very strongly then and feel strongly now that we have an obligation to subject our own actions and attitudes to an equivalent and critical moral scrutiny.

The impetus behind *One For The Road* was Pinter's concern for 'official torture subscribed to by so many governments. The other is the whole nuclear situation. I have been a member of CND for a number of years now.'

Within Pinter's work is a very deeply rooted pessimism, a sense of hopelessness, but one which is very allied, as he points out, to Samuel Beckett's statement 'You must go on, I can't go on, I'll go on.' Pinter says:

All we're talking about finally is what is real . . . There's only one reality, you know. You can interpret reality in various ways, but there's only one. That reality is thousands of people being tortured to death at this very moment, hundreds of thousands of megatons of nuclear bombs standing there waiting to go off at this very moment, then that's it, and that's that, it has to be faced.

In the play, Nicholas is in charge. Victor comes in, bruised, his clothes torn. Nicholas's first words to him include: 'You're a civilized man, so am I.' The title, *One For The Road*, is a phrase that Nicholas uses to punctuate the disquisition to Victor (who is far from being a victor). Nicholas keeps pouring himself drinks and resorting to the trappings of social convention. Victor's wife and son are kept somewhere else in the building. Presumably we are to believe that Victor has been tortured, and certainly Nicholas wants to make him and us believe his wife has been tortured as well. Behind him is the leader of the country who appeals to the patriotism of the majority, against which Victor in some way has transgressed. There is a blackout at the end.

In Act II Nicholas is with a small boy called Nicky, who has been taken away from his mother. The little boy has spat at soldiers and kicked them. It is a very calm little scene with an implication of great sinisterness behind it. In the next scene Nicholas is with the wife Gila; her clothes are torn and she is also bruised. The implication is that she has been raped. When she mentions her father, Nicholas rants about the father's loyalty to the regime against which she is transgressing. In the final scene Victor is now tidily dressed. It is implied that Victor's tongue or mouth have been damaged in some way.

What is interesting about this play is that although it is about the power of the torturer (in the sense that Nicholas controls the dynamic of every scene that he is in), it is also about the power of resistance, even though that power of resistance is a silent and relatively passive one. Victor reveals nothing, Gila reveals nothing, the child reveals nothing. They reveal their opposition by their silence. They do not use language to argue their position. The body may be tortured and abused, but the spirit is still able to resist.

Pinter's next play, *Mountain Language* (1988), was directed by the writer himself. A group of women wait outside a prison. One has been bitten by a dog. Army officers enter and abuse them, saying that the men have been imprisoned for using a mountain language which has been outlawed; only the city language is to be used. One of the women says that she doesn't speak the mountain language and that her husband is wrongfully imprisoned. The officers continue to abuse them.

In a brief second scene a woman tries to speak to a prisoner in the mountain language. A brief voice-over love scene between a young man and a woman follows.

The fourth scene, similarly brief, shows the guard telling the prisoner that the rules have been changed and his mother may speak in her language. When the prisoner tells her this she doesn't respond any more. Her language has been taken away. The sergeant's final words are: 'Look at this. You go out of your way to give them a helping hand and they fuck it up.'

The politicization of a younger generation of writers enabled an older generation (including Pinter) to develop more explicit links in their writing between politics and the imagination. *Mountain Language* is not just about torture; it is also about the way a people's culture is colonized, and when that happens their language and their very being is taken away. Without the ability to communicate there is nothing. The value and wonder of language is prized, all the more as Pinter's style becomes more and more spare and approaches silence, paradoxically as the content of his work becomes more politicized.

Differently placed from both Stoppard and Pinter is Edward Bond. Bond has always been vocal about his allegiance to pacifism, and one of his most famous plays, *Saved* (1965), sought to present an argument through the theatrically shocking spectacle of a baby being stoned to death by a group of disaffected youngsters. Bond homes in on issues he sees as morally vital to the healthy future of a society, and he symbolizes the importance of political choice through the dilemmas he sets up for his characters in the plays. His play *Lear* (1971) draws on violent imagery; its central symbol is a wall which represents the conflict between what Bond sees as 'natural' goodness and culturally produced 'evil'. Again and again Bond is drawn back to the situation of the individual, and his/her need to make positive choices to change their lives.

The Sea (1973) is set in 1907 on the English east coast. A cataclysmic scene opens the play with Willie seeking Colin in a dark sea after their boat has overturned. The second scene in a shop introduces Hatch, a paranoid draper, who believes in aliens from another planet. Evans, who is supposed to be the local fool and lives in a hut on the beach, is actually more sane than him. Willie goes to Evans to find out where Colin's body might have been washed up.

Bond continues his 1960s preoccupation with the nature of violence as a random act. Willie comes down to the beach with Rose, Colin's fiancée. Willie says:

> If you look at life closely it is unbearable, what people suffer, what they do to each other, how they hate themselves. Anything good is cut down and trodden on, the innocent and victims are like dogs, digging rats from a hole or an owl starving to death in the city. It is all unbearable, but that is where you have to find your strength. Where else is there?

They find Colin's body, and Rose goes off to get help. Hatch comes on carrying a knife. Willie hides from him. Hatch thinks the body is Willie's and stabs it repeatedly, in a random act of violence.

At the end there is a small note of optimism. Rose arrives and she and Willie are clearly about to leave together, in a rather abstractedly romantic ending. There is no real relationship between Rose and Willie, just an implied sense of bonding because of their previous relationships with Colin. Parochialism and suppressed irrational violence are linked in Bond's view to a particular kind of Englishness. The sensitive must leave to survive.

Pinter and Bond occupy a continuum of attitudes towards change. Where the former explores the experience of the trapped, from both sides, the latter focuses on the moment when individuals identify the need for change, and he implies that under whatever system, existential individuals can still make choices, however apparently insignificant, to improve their lot.

Finally, any account of the senior generation of playwrights would not be complete without reference to John McGrath, a transitional figure whose work spanned the concerns and methods of both pre- and post-1968. In 1971 McGrath founded, and was the main writer for and artistic director of, a touring company called 7:84. McGrath nailed his political colours to the post, in his allegiance with a left that sought to be more radical

Edward Bond

than the post-war Labour Party had become. The very title of the company was a reference to the fact that (at that time) seven per cent of the population owned eighty-four per cent of its wealth.

The company was based in Scotland, and from here toured to a carefully set up network of rural areas and urban working-class venues. McGrath himself had already become an adept and fluently popular writer, with episodes for one of the first television police series, *Z Cars*, and a powerful stage play about army life, *Events While Guarding the Bofors Gun* (1966). The plays, a vigorous mix of researched historical drama-documentary interspersed with dynamic rock music, were some of the most powerfully effective in the 1970s agitprop mould; entertaining, polemical and direct. Glasgow's socialist John McLean's life story was told in the form of a music-hall variety act in *The Game's A Bogey* (1974); *Out Of Our Heads* (1976) sought to deal with the personal problems of alcoholism in the unemployed, and *Little Red Hen* (1975) dramatized the debate between Scottish Nationalism and the Labour movement, using as a narrative device an engaging relationship between a feisty grandmother and her granddaughter, allowing McGrath the opportunity to respond – if largely only in a formal sense – to some of the critiques feminism was offering on the male-centredness of socialist theatre.

5

The world after 1968: Brenton, Edgar, Hare, Barker

The next generation of young writers was altogether more direct in its approaches to politics as subject matter. Although pacifism and the nature of individual moral choice had not disappeared from the broad intellectual and political agenda, they took a back seat in favour of the wave of socialist optimism in the late 1960s. In the theatre, in particular, this came via the influence of the plays and theories of Bertolt Brecht, whose work had become known in Britain during the 1950s, and whose 'theory of alienation', albeit scarcely ever examined in detail and sensitivity, was a major influence on the attitude of playwrights to the concept of character, motivation and social location.

Brecht's simple but clear insistence that the individual must be placed in his (sic) social and historical setting, was the major rationale behind many of the new kinds of political or history plays. These were not chronicles, as in the Shakespearean tradition, nor agitprop in form, like the campaigning touring pieces, but political morality plays, in the style of Brecht's own work. Brecht, of course, was aiming his work at a bourgeois audience which he was seeking to shock by giving them a theatre of ideas rather than emotions; the new playwrighting of the 1970s, staged as it was in the larger, established theatres, had as its audiences a mix of the bourgeoisie – the theatre-going public interested in new writing and the play of ideas – and an enthusiastic audience which already shared many of the views of the playwrights – indeed, from whose ranks the latter had emerged.

It is not surprising then that in all these plays a combination of elements appears. Many of the plays are set in epic sweeps of time (*Romans* by Howard Brenton moves from BC to 1980 AD, to take the most extreme example); hardly any of them give very much time to the kind of domestic setting (of whatever class) that so characterized the West End drawing room-based play. As a result of this, the working out of individual interpersonal relationships is squeezed out of the central space, with a curious consequence, as we shall see.

Of these playwrights, Brenton's preoccupation with violence as a moral as well as a political issue is closest to that of Edward Bond. His early apprenticeship mixed the individual and group approach, with his work with theatre groups such as Portable Theatre and the Brighton Combination in the late 1960s. He has also co-written plays (with David Hare; *Brassneck* (1973) about postwar political corruption, and *Sleeping Policemen*, with Tunde Ikoli, (1983)). His epic play, *Romans in Britain* (1980) managed to raise the spectre of censorship again when an (unsuccessful) action was taken out against it for incitement to obscenity because of its scene of attempted homosexual rape. Violence of all kinds – personal, political, physical and cultural – is the central driving theme of the piece, which begins in pre-Christian Britain. Celtish soldiers are on the run from the Romans. Three Druid boys find and murder one of them. In crude, staccato language, the play reveals a world of primitive brutality, at macro and micro-political level. The Romans recruit soldiers from the Druid farms. Everyone talks in the language of violence and there is very little to choose from between the different groupings, even though a Druid matriarch invites sympathy with her account of constant raids. An envoy, describing the Roman army smashing the woods and farms, tries to define them: 'A nation. What, a great family? No. A people? No. They are one huge thing.'

Roman soldiers enter and assault the Druid boys. One of the soldiers tries to rape a Druid boy, in a scene symbolic of imperialist domination. In the very next scene ordinary criminals kill a dog. Roman violence destroys the Druid spirit. One Druid, who was going to become a priest, says: 'We must have nothing to do with them, nothing. Abandon the life we know, change ourselves into animals.'

At the end of Part I, the Roman army advances with British army uniforms and equipment of the late 1970s. Part II moves between 515 AD and 1980 AD. It begins in modern times with Thomas Chichester, speaking in clipped upper-class tones, in a field, waiting. Chichester, an English soldier, disguised in farmworker's clothing, is set on by soldiers. As Chichester stays on stage, we then go back to 515 AD, the time of King Arthur. Chichester confronts a man he has been sent to assassinate,

Howard Brenton

O'Rourke, and says that because of what he sees in the fields (i.e., the play that we have seen so far), he wants to throw down his weapons. The Irish of course think he's mad, jeer at his liberalism and shoot him. At the very end we are left with Saxons telling the story of King Arthur, whose life is thought of as a golden age 'lost and yet to come'. The brutal present survives only because it can refer to a nostalgic view of history.

There is much cynicism and bitterness in Brenton's representation of history. If the presentation of unrelenting violence is intended to awaken the audience to anger against brutality, then this is mitigated by the pessimistic drive of the story which demonstrates very little success in resistance, virtually no effective resistance against military might, and defeat for those with any kind of vision. The strength of feeling that infuses the play's epic sweep is undoubtedly potent, and it is a play that provokes gut response rather than intellectual analysis.

David Edgar, on the other hand, the high point of whose success was his dramatisation of *Nicholas Nickleby* for the Royal Shakespeare Company in 1980, has, in his original work, taken on the mantle of dramatic historian for parts of the British Left. *Destiny* (1976) in particular, is a brave attempt to chart the roots of the political right wing within the depths of the British class system, and in a particular kind of male psyche. It opens in darkness with a speech from Nehru in 1947:

> A moment comes, which comes but rarely in history, when we step out from the old to the new, when an age ends, and when the soul of a nation, long oppressed, finds utterance.

At the end of World War II a new society is promised for the future. Three men – a soldier, Turner, a Colonel and Khera, an Indian – come from India to Britain where the Colonel, who is now very old (and speaks in rhyming couplets – a dramatic device to indicate an allegiance to the past) is dying.

In a drawing room, young Tory Peter Crosby discusses a bye-election, joking: 'Old Tories never die, they just get redistributed.' Peter's aunt, Mrs Chandler, defines the change taking place in England:

Once we stood for patriotism, Empire. Now it's all sharp
young men, with coloured shirts and cockney accents
reading *The Economist*.

The scene moves to the Labour Club where Clifton and his
wife Sandy are playing darts. Sandy's wifely (and dramatic) role
is to ask questions about politics, to which Clifton knows the
answers. Next follows a view of the future from an old-style
Conservative, Major Rolfe:

> . . . it's not true we've lost an Empire, haven't found a
> role. We have a role. As Europe's whipping boy . . . And
> for those – the people that I come from – that is a
> betrayal.

Turner (in 1970) runs an antique shop with a Tory poster
on the wall, and he rejoices at 'an end to six years of Socialist
misrule'. A young man called Tony works for him. Razak,
a property-owning Pakistani with a Cockney accent, is about
to turf Turner out of his shop, and he speaks directly to the
audience:

> So told him. Idea was to conceal a whole row being bought
> by one developer . . . But nothing he could do, and liked
> his face, so told him.

This effective rhetorical style excludes the personal pronoun
'I'. This represents not just the stiff-upper-lip middle class,
but also the exclusion of the individual, the subjective, and
the notion of psychological or individual motivation. It is as
if the impersonal dramatic style here operates at the expense
of the personal, the subjective, and the sexual, as becomes
clear later.

The play dissects the relationship of the far Right to
Conservatism:

> Beware the man – the Right Conservative, the disillusioned
> military man – who'd take the Socialism out of National
> Socialism. But also, even more, beware the man – the
> passionate young man who would take the National out of
> National Socialism.

David Edgar

In the scenes where the far Right is represented, the women serve tea, take messages. Women at a public meeting represent the ordinary concerns of family, schools and homes.

The significant political issues and ideas are fought out by men: the rise of the new Right, an impending strike, and the contradictions of class and race. The women are silent servicers, the passive voice of personal life, or, at their apex in the persona of Sandy, the detached voice of momentary conscience. The political is seen to happen between men, while the personal is merely referred to by the presence of women. The two spheres are held separate.

While this is a reflection of social reality, it is presented with virtually no comment or irony. Indirectly, therefore, it also operates as an assertion about the very nature of political activity itself, and of the priorities that current politics (right and left) gives to issues which preoccupy men in particular. Thus a play which takes a deeply responsible attitude to the development of political ideas, does so (not necessarily with overt conscious intent) in terms of male social being. There is no inclusion of either co-operation or conflict between men and women. The gender hierarchy is a pre-feminist one. My aim in making this kind of analysis is not to castigate Edgar's (or any other playwright's) imagination for being gender determined, but to demonstrate what I take to be the fact that the imagination of each individual will be formed by a combination of nature and nurture: the class they are born into, their race and gender, their education and the ideas and beliefs they consciously espouse.

The debates about gender relations, raised so eloquently by feminism, have, of course, influenced male writers whose concerns include a sensitivity to inequality and oppression, but at the same time, this does not necessarily mean that the imaginative worlds which they refract in their plays will be devoid of deeply rooted patterns of thought. This male-centredness continues to be evinced in Edgar's works.

Maydays (1983) opens on May Day 1945. Jeremy Crowther, aged seventeen, a member of the Young Communist League, is celebrating the victory of a Labour government.

We then move on to 1956 and the Hungarian uprising, where Lermontov and a female stenographer represent the Russian army trying to put down the rebellion. We return to 1962 and Crowther who is now a schoolmaster at a minor public school. Seventeen-year-old Martin Glass, a young rebel, wears a CND badge.

Martin and Jeremy strike a chord of sympathy over CND, Jeremy remembering his radical past. Jeremy had left the Communist Party over Hungary, and he comments in recollection of those who struggled in the 1930s:

> And what we'd missed, of course, was all the glory. And indeed the confidence that once you'd cracked the shackles of the system, every man indeed would be an Aristotle or a Michelangelo. Because in a way, it had already happened. And it hadn't turned out how we thought it would at all. Oh, it was decent, sure, and reasonably caring in its bureaucratic way . . . But you realise there's something missing. The working class is freer than it's ever been . . .
>
> But somewhere . . . you hear a kind of scream. The scream of the possessed. And you realise there's all the difference in the world between liberty and liberation.

Despite its cynical sadness, these are the sentiments that the male playwright generation of the mid-1950s and the early 1960s were also exploring. Martin's youthful idealism counterpoints Crowther: where Jeremy looks to the past, Martin looks to the future.

Martin is in California in 1967 with the hippies and the draft resisters. In May 1968, he is very much in the thick of British student protest, living in a Midlands commune where in the living room there is a washing line with nappies, and a man stencilling: politics represented via a visual image at work at home as well as out on the streets.

In Moscow Lermontov is changing his ideas. Originally he thought the invasion of Hungary was right, but now he believes it was a mistake and is trying to get people to sign a petition. He believes in ideals but not in brutal practices. Back in London there is a student occupation at Leeds University where Jeremy is teaching. In 1970, during the invasion of Cambodia, Martin joins a left-wing group called Socialist Vanguard: 'I want to be a traitor to my class.' The personal is subsumed into the political for Martin. In 1972 Martin visits Jeremy:

| *Jeremy*: | Oh, is there a Mrs Glass? |
| *Martin*: | The Party. |

One of the debates running through the play is the
distinction, if any, between a subjective and an objective
position. Jeremy comments about another member of the group:
'He may think he is a revolutionary. Objectively he is nothing
of the kind.' And he then comments to Martin that he 'couldn't
care less what you feel, it's what you think and do'. Martin is
expelled from the party for not thinking or doing the correct
things, and for apparently feeling things that are in conflict with
his political allegiance.

At the end of the Vietnam war in 1975, Martin is going
through yet another crisis of conscience.

> And as once again the proofs pile up that we are
> catastrophically wrong, we change the position . . . that
> all the stillbirths, all the monstrous misbegottens with no
> legs or stomachs but with all those twitching ears and
> beady little eyes, that they're the deviation and that *therefore*
> somewhere in the future there must be a norm.

The introduction of convincing personal motivation comes
when Lermontov, who has been imprisoned as a dissident,
encounters the woman stenographer who had betrayed him
in the first scene. Clara, the stenographer, says she did it
because he sneered at her for being an ignorant peasant girl.
He comments: 'But what was visited on me broke all the
rules . . . It was sharp and real and *personal*.'

In an imaginative moment that recalls the outsider figures
of the 1950s/1960s, it is the foreigners, the strangers, between
whom the really personal gestures take place. It is not just
an illustration that people in the Soviet Union can act out of
personal motivation, but it is a displacement of subjective
personal motivation from the British political arena to a
foreign one.

At the end, Martin travels, if not quite a full circle, then
certainly back to something like his parents' views, and ends up
working for a Tory think-tank.

Politics is presented in two strands in the play. There are
the sets of political arguments through which Martin moves

and in relation to which he struggles all the time; the dynamic
of the action follows his story. Then there is the off-centre
character of Amanda who never engages intellectually with
any issue. Amanda is one political move ahead of Martin,
which gives her an apparent importance in 'leading' his
politics. Yet she does so without debate, 'instinctively', as it
were, giving her an overwhelmingly important metaphorical
significance. This may look as if it is a chivalric image
of the power of women to lead change, but it is a power
with no social base. It happens without conscious control,
so that rebellion itself becomes an infantile disorder, the
correlative being that when rebels grow up they have to leave
idealism behind (as Martin does and as Jeremy did during
his time).

Of these two approaches to politics, the intellectual/
conceptual is given greater value. The world of politics 'belongs'
to the men, and women are not given any politics, even on the
left. Feminism is fleetingly referred to, but it is not part of the
visible fabric of Amanda's life. The potency of this play, with
its vigorous intellectual demands, shows the way ideas impinge
on people's lives, but works by denying its characters, male and
female, space for emotional/sexual entanglements, with a vision
of heroism in which men monopolize politics and the women
service or symbolize the continuity of hope and the paradoxical
vanity of protest.

The male-centredness of this kind of implicit definition of
the nature of politics also permeates the work of playwright
David Hare, whose approach to the modern history play
involves a particularly powerful focus on the important
institutions of ruling class power. This is true even of an early,
all-female cast play, *Slag* (1970), which features Joanne (23), Elise
(26), and Ann (32). The title carries reverberations of the slag
heap, i.e., the waste thrown out of a coal mine. 'Slag' is also a
slang term of sexual abuse applied to women.

The play is set in a small girls' public school which has
only seven pupils left. In the common room, the women led by
Joanne vow to:

abstain from all forms of varieties of sexual intercourse . . .
To keep my body in order to register my protest against
the way our society is run by men for men whose aim

is the subjugation of the female and the enslavement of
the working woman . . . in order to work towards the
establishment of a truly socialist society.

A vow of celibacy, feminist protest against male domination,
and the desire for socialism, are presented as a version of
modern feminism. Ann's aim is different – a late 1960s
libertarianism:

> We will build a new sort of school where what people
> feel for people will be the basis of their relationship. No
> politics.

Elise, by contrast, is all conventional femininity, concerned
with her looks and her innate sexual magnetism. She speaks of
'the great rush of air to my legs that sucks men to me'.

The women inhabit a hermetic society; the school is going
to the dogs; parents are taking their pupils away. From the
beginning we see women lose more and more control of a
public institution. This is marked by the continual reference
throughout the text to a dog which craps everywhere, as
well as to the bickering, the names the women call each
other and the way they systematically try to demolish one
another.

Joanne's ideas of 'women being really women' means
celibacy. She claims that 'masturbation is the only form of
sexual expression left to the authentic woman'. Joanne is
someone whose 'feminism', confused as it is, is identified with
escapism and a fear of sexuality. In addition, whenever Joanne
expresses any of her principles for a harmonious community
of women, she is theoretically undermined, as the others play
violent practical jokes on her.

The women enact sado-masochistic versions of male/female
sexual games. In this oddly abandoned family Ann is the
mother figure, Joanne the bullying and brutal father and Elise
the vulnerable and submissive child. The 'home' is an institution
which is falling apart, an irony considering Joanne's claims that
she has 'left everything I loved' in order to find 'a different way
of life'. The world of the cinema, with which she is obsessed,
represents the world of men, the world which she claims to
have abandoned.

Joanne's hostility to sexuality and motherhood (she says she is a virgin) are expressed in a dream about Elise, who claims to be pregnant:

> You lay down on the table and the first animal came out.
> There was some discussion among us as to who should
> have the first bite, but a man interrupted and ate your first
> child which was a chicken. The second was a fish and I
> had some. You lay on the table and the wet animals came
> regularly from you. And we all ate.

Both Ann and Elise still need and yearn for men, and their relationship (non-sexual, we presume) with each other is an unhappy substitute. Ann and Elise at least have some kind of friendship, whereas Joanne is isolated all the way through from female friendship. Feminism is represented as non-sexual and indeed in many respects anti-sexual, as something undesirable and repulsive, to be done violence to. Women are represented, through Joanne and in the world of this disintegrating public school, as incapable of choosing art or the creations of the mind, horrific, frustrated when they try to choose the pleasures of the body, and certainly incapable of institutional power.

The framework of the play suggests a satire on the public school system, its mores, its hermeticism and irrelevance to the modern world. Elise comments: 'There was no virgin birth, there are simply declining standards in private education and that is all.'

The satire is conveyed through the representation of relationships between women, and in the relationship between one woman who claims to be a feminist and two who are not. In the process of unravelling the metaphors, these two objective correlatives are themselves demolished. Women are shown to be incapable of running anything, of having any real power, or if they do have power it is not a power which they can sustain. None of them really has any pride in her work, and feminism is shown to be muddled at best, tragic at worst, and usually somewhere in between; pathetic, brutal and abortive.

The play has an articulate, compulsive power about it, driven by the educated and sardonic language which moves fast, even when very little is actually happening on stage; the language itself constitutes the satirical dynamic.

David Hare

Teeth 'n' Smiles (1975) is set during one night in June 1968.
The opening image is a romantic one:

> ARTHUR is lying on one bench, staring. He is wearing
> a silver top hat and a silk scarf, but the effect is oddly
> discreet. He is tall, thin and twenty-six.

Arthur is charismatic and immaculately dressed. Gradually the
cast congregates; Laura, who cooks and sews and services the
pop group who have come up to play at a Cambridge May Ball,
describes Maggie:

> She starts drinking at breakfast, she passes out after lunch,
> then she's up for supper ready for the show. Then after
> the show she starts drinking. At two-thirty she's out
> again. Morning she gets up. And drinks. She is a great
> professional. Never misses a show.

Laura is the 'straight guy' in this play, while all the men
are eccentric and interesting characters. Laura is a mixture of
office manager, personnel manager and wardrobe mistress.
Arthur was at Cambridge, so is in a position to sneer at the
current crop of undergraduates. He delivers a monologue
about how he first met Maggie when she was sixteen, an
uneducated folk singer. In Svengali fashion he made her into
the extraordinary singer that she is; but their relationship has
gone sour.

When Maggie first appears she shows her power through
song. The songs that she sings are written by Arthur, so that
through her singing she gives birth to his voice and to his art.
Even though they no longer have a relationship, he lives on for
her in his songs.

There is a division here between the creative mind
that produces the words and music, and the emotional
expression from the interpretive artist: the man provides the
words to articulate the woman's emotions – i.e. the man
speaks for the woman, and enables her to speak in his voice;
he is intellect, she emotion. Where Arthur is immaculate
and articulate in his physical and mental control, Maggie
is articulate in her lack of control. Of her promiscuity,
she says:

I only sleep with very stupid men . . . they never
understand a word I say. That makes me trust them . . . So
each one gets told a different secret, some terrible piece of
my life that only they will know . . . Then the day I die,
every man I've known will make for Wembley stadium.
And each in turn will recount his special bit. And when
they are joined, they will lighten up the sky.

Maggie is an anguished artist who uses music as a way
of interpreting the pain of her own fragmentation. Laura
comments:

It's just possible anywhere, any time, to decide to be
a tragic figure. It's just an absolute determination to go
down. The reasons are arbitrary, it may almost be pride,
just not wanting to be like everyone else. I think you
can die to avoid cliché. And you can let people die to
avoid cliché.

Maggie's isolation is essential to the plot: at the end she
becomes the willing scapegoat for the band, who hide all their
drugs in her bag. When the police raid the place, it is she who is
arrested.

The men retain control over their environment, whereas
Maggie in the end loses control of hers. Arthur comments:

Her problem is: she's frightened of being happy. And if
ever it looked as if she might make it, if the clouds cleared
and I, or some other man, fell perfectly into place, if
everyone loved her and the music came good, that's when
she'd kill herself.

There is ambiguity here. The tragedy of Maggie's
position is continually undermined in comparison with
Arthur the charismatic commentator, a guru for Maggie
and the group, sexually attractive and always immaculate.
He is never physically damaged by his environment, while
Maggie has always just changed into a dress or is about to
change out of one. She is physically a mess, she has to be
carried round by the men; she carries decay around with her
on stage.

Certainly it is a very potent image, one which is carried through even more powerfully here by the use of rock music with Maggie as the central voice for the band's art and Arthur's message. This voice has to be destroyed for the sake of Arthur's creativity – he can watch with a writer's eye as she gradually dissipates – and for an imagination which has to destroy the creature it has created lest it get out of control – the Frankenstein syndrome.

The man as artist is vindicated and he will have to find another woman to interpret his art. It is more of an early nineteenth-century romantic notion about the nature of creativity than something born out of 1968. The articulate satire about the privilege of the Cambridge education system is telling and effective, but it operates also as a buffer against the personal vulnerabilities of the men who appropriate women as metaphors or servants in order to survive. And in particular, the emotional potency of the music carries the play's main emotional message, with its willing female sacrifice at the centre. Certainly the major central female role is a real challenge for an actress, but it is used in a post-censorship context to reassert pre-feminist images about the relative male sphere of creator, and the female sphere of interpreter. With an additional bitter twist: where the romantic image leaves the female muse pure and undefiled, in the 1970s, the independent woman is a danger, and must be imaginatively destroyed for art (i.e., male creativity) to survive.

The playwright in whom scatology and sexual imagery is most directly applied to the corruptibility (as he sees it) of political institutions, is Howard Barker. Unlike Edward Bond, who has continued to remain faithful to the principle of individual moral choice, Barker creates a world full of amoral people. The individual, in his stage plays, is merely a scaled-down version of the amoral drive for power demonstrated through institutions. In *The Hang of the Gaol*, a tough and bitter play, British society is symbolized by a prison which has been burned to the ground. Barker's cynicism knows no party boundaries; the Home Secretary in the ensuing enquiry is Labour; the ordinary people are represented as no better than their oppressors. His language is powerful, never shying from unpleasant physical imagery, and although the major characters in his plays are almost always male, he at least creates female characters who are as violent and cynical as their male counterparts. His is the drama of profound cynicism, conveyed through a gutsy, invigorating and shocking use of language. This implies hope for cultural energy as the saviour of social relations, even where politics fails.

6

Sexuality and gender: Lowe, Sherman, Gay Sweatshop, Churchill, O'Malley, Gems, Dunn, Page

As has been seen, the exploration and new interest in sexuality and gender roles which was prompted by feminism had an indirect effect on many male playwrights. While both David Hare and David Edgar clearly struggled with the combination of fascination with, and resistance to, the importance of women and sexuality, others have taken a rather different approach. Two of these, one dealing with male heterosexuality and one with male homosexuality, were particularly poignant and emotionally daring.

Tibetan Inroads by Stephen Lowe (1981) is set in Tibet. Dorja, a young Tibetan man, has an affair with a young woman married to an old landowner. The affair is discovered and in feudal society the punishment is severe. Dorja is arrested by his Buddhist monk brother, found guilty, deprived of his property and castrated as punishment for having stolen another man's wife. After the operation he has to redefine himself as a man, when he is no longer able to do so through a conventional macho sexual self-image. He continues to experience desire: 'They said I'd never feel like this again. I can't do anything. I'm not a man, I can't feel like a man.' The pain he expresses demonstrates the paradox of pain and triumph, that whatever happens to the body, the imagination can continue to work.

In the second part of the play, Chinese revolutionaries enter Tibet. A parallel is drawn between Dorja's sexual desire and the political desires of the new army, his frustration and their fulfilment. He becomes a labourer:

> I work on the road, but I work like a donkey not like a man. My mind is full of dreams. I do not ask myself all the time who is this road for. Is it for the people . . . I should ask these questions more often and out loud so that my comrades can help me in answering them.

The play, through its complex and subtle central character, demonstrates that social change cannot happen without desire and the imagination. Dorja's castration, the traditional act of unmanning, does nothing of the sort. His body is damaged but his intellectual and social powers are not. Sexual potency and political power do not have to be synonymous.

At the same time, the individual is presented as a tragic victim of a social system, and finally, in a poignancy unusual in the drama of this period, it is demonstrated that while political systems can be changed, biological characteristics (i.e., the gendered body) are immutable.

Bent by Martin Sherman (1979) is set in Berlin in the 1930s, where the Nazis are beginning to take power. Max, a homosexual, is arrested and taken to a prison camp. He claims he is Jewish in order not to be accused of being a homosexual, and is given a yellow star. He becomes friendly with another person, Horst, who wears a pink triangle, the symbol of a homosexual. The two prisoners work together. As they stand to attention during every rest period there is an erotic exchange as both characters, looking out front on stage, make love using only words. Max says: 'We can't look at each other, we can't touch.' Horst says: 'We can feel . . . each other without touching.' The two make love through words with desire and actuality related and separated. The taboo and the possible are both made explicit in one theatrical moment.

At the end of the play, Horst is killed and Max then touches him for the first time. As a result of this, Max is prepared to take on his real identity, to 'come out', even though he knows the consequences. He walks voluntarily into an electric fence and dies. The theme of homosexual persecution is highlighted because of the double nature of the taboo, both in normal society and in the concentration camp, and the deeply personal act of sexuality is conveyed in the horrendously depersonalized context of the camp. It is a play of extraordinary power.

Bent was an internationally successful play, given impetus by the gay movement here and in the US. At grass roots level, a number of touring companies concentrated on the experiences of gay people, most prominently through the work of a company called Gay Sweatshop, founded in 1974. At first largely men, they were soon joined by women. In some plays they worked together, in other plays separately, producing sometimes all–women plays and other times all–male plays. A first season of lunchtime plays called *Homosexual Acts* was staged in London, and throughout the 1970s and 1980s Gay Sweatshop continued to produce plays at regular intervals.

The Dear Love of Comrades by Noel Greig, chronicles the relationship between Edward Carpenter and E. M. Forster. The play is framed within the context of a radio talk in the 1940s by E. M. Forster, to whom the Carpenter menage was an important way of finding himself and his own sexuality. The play is set in the 1890s, showing how characters were influenced by the Oscar Wilde trial and the rise of the Independent Labour Party. Edward Carpenter, one of the leading lights of the early socialist movement in Britain, declared his homosexuality, and the play sought to bring his life and times back into public prominence.

Any Woman Can (1975) was the first play from Gay Sweatshop about women. The central character, Ginnie, uses the stage as a public platform to confront the audience with the taboo figure of a lesbian to challenge their prejudices: 'I'm here to stay, to infiltrate, to convert.' She summons up figures from her life, and they punctuate her monologue. A vicious headmistress appears. Ginnie confides in the audience about prejudice against her at boarding school and hostility from the other girls; suicide attempts; her first affairs; a relationship with a woman whose boyfriend takes her away. She begins to meet other lesbians. She explains that it is not just sex, it has to do with women being friends, since women are more important to her than men. She goes to a gay bar and is picked up by an older woman. She moves through a series of relationships. The play ends with a number of monologues from different women. It is not a morality play, and not a romantic narrative play with a happy ending. It is a demonstration piece, designed to reassure lesbians in the audience that they are not alone, and to show – poignantly and defiantly – that being lesbian is only one of a number of options.

However, the most incisive inroads made in bringing an important area of experience centre stage has been in the work of women playwrights. Many of these have mixed feelings about being dubbed 'feminist' or being tagged with the label 'woman writer'. However one uses these labels, what is undeniable is that the wave of playwrights – both older and younger generations – would not have emerged without a climate of feminist discussion to enable them to take the difficult step of deciding to write for the theatre.

Of these, three women from the pre-1968 generation have made a particular impact. However, the fact of their being an older generation does not mean that they have anything like the same track record as their male counterparts. For Caryl Churchill, Pam Gems and Nell Dunn (the latter primarily a book writer who turned late to theatre) the real change in their writing careers came at the beginning of the 1970s, spurred by more militant, younger women. Pam Gems was involved with the first Women's Theatre Festival in London in 1973, and later went on to write for both the fringe and for the Royal Shakespeare Company. Caryl Churchill had had a number of plays broadcast on radio, and after the production of *Owners* at the Royal Court Theatre in 1972, became more and more influenced by the kinds of discussions and ways of working practised by Monstrous Regiment and Joint Stock (See chapter 3). Her successful working relationship with director Max Stafford-Clark has given her a commanding position, with the kind of access to production at the Royal Court that enabled her to develop steadily as a stylist.

The two plays written and produced during 1976 show both aspects of her interest in class-based politics. *Vinegar Tom,* with its focus on the persecution of women as 'witches' during the seventeenth century, weaves ideas about women as outsiders, and about superstition and ignorance in a world where both working and privileged women are seen as victims if they don't conform to society's expectations. *Light Shining in Buckinghamshire* took a more formal look at the politics and religious conflicts of the English Civil War. Here too, individuals who are not seen as necessary by the politicians are destroyed, and as an almost direct tribute to the research process, chunks of the Putney Debates on power are interpolated wholesale into the structure of the play.

In *Cloud Nine* (1979) Churchill, again working with Joint Stock, explored gender in both a thematic and a theatrical fashion. The play, split in time between the nineteenth and twentieth centuries, plays with the infinite possibilities of the unities. The first half traces a conventional British colonial family: patriarchal, women kept in their place, the sexual double standard maintained, and any non-heterosexual desires strictly suppressed. The second half takes the same characters and catapults them forward in time, to demonstrate the different sexual and gender freedoms in the late twentieth century. Here a grown man plays a girl of four, demonstrating the absurdities of gender stereotyping, and also by implication subverting and appropriating the cross-dressing conventions in British theatre so embedded in the pantomime tradition.

Top Girls (1982) opens with a semi-surreal scene in a restaurant, a public space out of time, where Marlene is celebrating having been made managing director of an employment agency. She has invited five female characters from history and mythology. They talk to, at and across each other about their pasts, husbands, lovers and the children they have had or lost. The ups and downs of their lives are enumerated and exchanged, and Marlene toasts them: 'We've come a long way. To our courage and the way we changed our lives and our extraordinary achievements.'

The rest of the play moves between Marlene's life as a successful career woman, and that of her sister Joyce in the country. Marlene has competed for a job with a man and won, leaving him pathetic and broken. Angie, ostensibly Joyce's daughter, comes to visit Marlene in London unexpectedly. She suspects that Marlene might be her mother, and in fact we discover in the final long, very powerfully written scene between the two sisters, she is right.

The two women have made different life choices. Joyce stayed in the country, whereas Marlene moved to London and became successful. Marlene hasn't seen Angie since the girl was nine. Marlene accuses Joyce of being jealous because she was the clever one. Joyce responds directly: 'I don't know how you could leave your own child.' Joyce was not able to have children, so each woman has in fact got what she wanted.

Marlene supports Margaret Thatcher and economic policies like monetarism, and is relatively promiscuous. She believes in the individual, where Joyce believes in a much more collective class viewpoint. The argument between the two sisters is not resolved. The choices each woman has made are presented as equally valid. It is not a play which celebrates bourgeois success and nor one which campaigns for working-class

Caryl Churchill

loyalty to its origins, and in that sense it is quite apolitical in attributing values to either position. But it illustrates a lively, taut relationship between the two sisters; in this one scene of kinship relationship the real emotional tensions, conflicts and interpersonal contact is shown. Motherhood is shown as just one option for women, with no value judgement applied in the play. In this it does not seem to cause any problems for Marlene, certainly not as far as she is allowed to experience. These existential women represent new possibility.

In 1977 Mary O'Malley's play *Once A Catholic* achieved success, beginning at the Royal Court and moving to the West End. It is set in a convent school in 1956–7. While Jimmy Porter was rebelling in Osborne's *Look Back In Anger*, good Catholic girls in Willesden were being taught to become wives and mothers. Inadvertently one becomes a rebel. Mary Mooney is the only seriously religious girl, but somehow becomes a scapegoat through her very innocence, her simplicity. The nuns try to give the girls euphemistic sex education lessons. A box of Tampax is carried onto the stage when one of the nuns finds it in the girls' toilets. The play is witty and moving about a growing up process, in a way which avoids clichés.

This play is itself a rites of passage piece; as women's experiences begin slowly to become subject matter for drama, this has been one of the first points of call, much in the way that first novels are often rites of passage works for their authors. This is continued in the work of the younger generation of women writers, such as Sharman McDonald. Her *When I Was A Girl I Used to Scream and Shout* (1984) opens on a beach, where Morag has taken her daughter Fiona away on holiday. The play uses a flashback to the 1950s. Vari stayed at home and married. Fiona left home and became independent.

Pam Gems' play *Piaf* (1978), based on the life of the French cabaret singer, is a chronicle play. On the stage, Piaf takes us through her life from the very beginning, as she climbs her way up the show-business ladder from street singer. She has free relationships with men; her language is rough. Action is punctuated with songs, giving Piaf the freedom to move between public performance and private life, despite the fact that one man friend advises her to keep the public and private separate. But Piaf cannot separate the persona and the performance. For her there is no distinction. The play follows her though a bad car crash, addiction to heroin, and a cynicism about the exploitation of show business. Despite everything, she remains true to her working-class origins. And in the final scene, a bitter-sweet romantic ending, she has a young lover who looks after her and her longstanding woman friend Toine.

A more social-realistic play, *Steaming* by Nell Dunn (1981), is set in a Turkish baths. Here too, frankness about sexual relationships and sexuality is inherent. Taboo is exposed onstage. The privacy of women's physicality is no longer totally excluded from the action, and a kaleidoscopic view of female kind is presented through the various characters. Violet, who manages the baths, is a mother figure. Josie is a bright sparky woman obsessed with sex and her latest violent lover. Mrs Meadows, an eccentric old woman, and her daughter Dawn, live in slum conditions. There are also two middle-class women, Nancy and Jane.

We learn about their lives as they talk to each other and argue. The plot as such is fairly minimal – whether or not there is hot water, whether the baths are to be closed. No men take part in the central action. Finally, as the baths are about to be closed, the women decide to occupy the building in a Utopian symbol of resistance and vulnerability, demonstrating a brief solidarity on territory which is about to be taken away from them.

Such plays with all-female casts and women at the centre of the action reveal new sets of preoccupations with the relationship between the public and private, with specific reference to the experiences of women. All the plays in some form present women in groups. But they also introduce woman as an individual, not an atomized heroine at the centre of the play or a metaphor for men's angst and conscience. They present women as the subject of drama and mistresses of their own destinies. In this context, traditional concepts of dramatic conflict are underemphasized, in the interests of breaking the taboo and presenting women as a valid subject matter for drama.

Louise Page's *Tissue* (1978) was also influenced by its cast and director, women who had been involved with feminism and with the role of women. Sally has breast cancer. The opening scene presents clichés which are then explored to reveal the feelings beneath them: 'All this fuss over a pound of flesh.' 'It's not a functional organ after all.' 'Why me?' 'It's only a bit of tissue.' Only one character is named: Sally herself. The other two are simply designated as 'Man' and 'Woman'.

Here too there are flashbacks to the way in which Sally is brought up by a mother who was embarrassed to refer to her breasts and who didn't want her to touch her body with her hands. Sally is obsessed with wondering whether she smells. And although here the reference is to a smell in the septic wound, the worry becomes an emblem of the way women are constantly encouraged to hide body odour. The play functions as a documentary account of the woman's experience as a cancer patient, with a thorough (almost by numbers) examination about women's mixed attitudes to their own bodies.

In Page's *Golden Girls* (1984) a women's amateur athletics team trains to take a gold medal in the Olympic Games. This play is structured in a succession of short, fast-moving schematic scenes. A woman doctor provides expositional information about the sports world and drugs, punctuated by more personal moments such as one of the athletes looking for her favourite teddy bear.

The plot concerns how far the women will be prepared to go in the interests of winning. Will they take a drug if assured by the doctor that it will not show up in tests? The structuring of *Golden Girls* is adroit and cool. Interpersonal relationships are glanced across but not explored. Page's terse style attempts to draw together social and private worlds, but remains rooted in its documentary origins, and its often elliptical dialogue operates both to suggest subtext and to conceal emotion.

7

Comments from the margin: Wesker Friel, Matura

If politics provided the major agenda for many male writers, one which has been confronted and developed in turn by feminist and gay perspectives, both these forces for new ideas and new writing have been further enriched by ethnic voices. These have come from older groups like the Scots (see John McGrath, chapter 4), the Irish or the Jewish community, or from newer ethnic groups, challenging the centre from the margin.

In every generation there are some playwrights whose work has had a strong impact at certain points, but whose careers have then wavered. One such is Arnold Wesker, whose work is appreciated and performed far more in other countries than it is here; an ironic situation for someone whose trilogy of plays about a Jewish Communist family had such acclaim and success during the 1960s.

Although Wesker's work has dealt with a variety of themes, he remains Britain's only regularly staged Jewish playwright. His play *Shylock* began life as *The Merchant* in 1976. Wesker wrote the play in response to two productions of Shakespeare's *The Merchant of Venice*, one featuring Laurence Olivier as Shylock in Jonathan Miller's 1973 production at the National Theatre, the other John Barton's 1981 production. Wesker sets his version of Shakespeare's story in a Jewish ghetto in Venice in 1563.

Shylock is in his study cataloguing manuscripts with the help of his friend Antonio, a merchant. He owns Hebrew books which are officially banned, and is admired by Antonio whose life is devoted to trade. Shylock invites Antonio to stay the night, even though it is illegal for gentiles to stay in the ghetto.

Portia has arrived to put her father's estate back in order. Portia is educated, a woman not merely destined for wife and motherhood. Jessica, Shylock's daughter, is fed up with books although she respects scholarship: 'There is a world outside the covers of a book, isn't there? Men don't always behave as philosophers fear, do they?' She believes there is 'only chaos and misery and in it we must carve out just sufficient order for an ounce of happiness. Because the world is full of madmen writing books.'

When Antonio asks Shylock to lend him money, and suggests drawing up a contract, Shylock doesn't think friends need a contract. Antonio says: 'The law demands it, no dealings may be made with Jews unless by a legal bond,' to which Shylock responds: 'That law was made for enemies not friends.' Shylock gets angry and insists that he should take the money, but there will be no bond, no collateral and no time limit, for the sake of friendship. Because Antonio insists on keeping the law, Shylock insists on making 'a nonsense bond'. And that is the origin of the bond for a pound of flesh. They join in amusement, tickling each other.

Wesker is writing about the possibilities of friendship across cultural differences. He argues:

> You have us for life, gentlemen, for life. Learn to live with us. The Jew is the Christian's parent. Difficult I know. Parent/children relationships are always difficult. And even worse when murder is involved within the family. But what can we do? It is the family. Not only would I be your friend but I have to be your friend.

But while Shylock wants to talk philosophy and theology, the others want to talk about trade and political power, and in the end economic exigencies are shown to cut across desires for friendship. Antonio's ship has sunk, and he tells Shylock he cannot raise the money. Shylock says they will be allowed to drop the bond, and Antonio, who believes in the rule of law, says they mustn't. The court is in fact prepared, hypocritically, to release both parties from the need to see the contract through. But Shylock now refuses, with a mixture of pride and stubbornness. His contempt for the double standards of an anti-semitic society rehabilitates him as a figure in imaginative history.

Wesker's early plays – particularly his Kahn family trilogy – took serious cognizance of the roles of women. This later became more self-consciously singled out in a series of one-woman plays.

In *Yardsale* (1985), Stephanie, a schoolteacher in her late forties, comes home and discovers a letter saying that her husband has gone off with someone else after 25 years, on the grounds that their relationship is over and he needs surprise. Her three children have left home. She is alone. She speaks to a friend on the phone. She goes to an art gallery. She eats alone in a restaurant. She goes to a bookshop. Finally she goes to a car boot sale.

The monologue is a study of the surface symptoms of loneliness and isolation. We don't learn much about the past, only that she never got anything out of her sexual relationship. The main motif is that of theft:

> I've invested in you my youth, my womanhood, the secrets of my body, my fund of love, friendship, wisdom and patience, and my investments should be showing a return, damn it. I should be plucking the profits by now . . . . But you have taken them and run off with them, snatched them from under my nose to share with someone else.

The play ends with a wistful 'I can steal things', but she remains among the debris of a relationship that's over, with postcards, cushions, boxes full of bits and pieces that mean everything to the people they belong to but come to mean nothing when they are in the anonymity of a sale.

Whatever Happened to Betty Lemon (1986) is about an elderly disabled woman. A letter arrives nominating her as 'handicapped woman of the year' and this prompts an outburst revealing some of the reality beneath her public life as wife of Sir James Lemon, socialist MP for Birmingham North. The most vivid dramatic aspect of the piece is the game she plays with her electric wheelchair, and a noose that hangs in the room. They are objects that declare her resilience, her refusal to be quiet, to lie down and be old and empty.

Annie Wobbler (1983) is a 'part-time tramp, part-time cleaning woman'; she is dressed in voluminous clothes and keeps her mug, plate and knife in the folds of her skirt. The monologue is set in 1939. She begins: 'They tell me I smell. I don't smell nothing, madam. But then no one don't know nothing about themselves, do they.' The monologue is addressed to a madam offstage. Annie is a gentile cleaner who has worked

Arnold Wesker

for Jewish families. Her view of the world is full of the detail of daily life: 'Not the way I was taught to make tea. Never use twice boiled water, my first madam said, you boil the goodness away. Fresh water, heat the pot, a spoonful for each person. One for his nob, and then leave.' She just is what she is, 'a serving maid for other people, a bag of rags and bones'. She can't read or write.

This old woman is transformed into a much younger 'Anna', wearing black underwear, a young graduate preparing to go out on a date. She reels off a catalogue of the man's faults, but as she makes up and dresses, her final parting shot is information that he's her first date since she got her degree.

She in turn is transformed into Annabella Wharton, a successful middle-aged novelist. A voice-over (actually her own voice) interviews her, about her fourth successful novel. She reveals herself selfconsciously to be

> a mid culture writer. I give people the impression I'm treating them intellectually without actually calling their intellect into play. People feel much more comfortable with that sort of work, which is why I've got all this attention.

She has no man, no children. It is a performance in which she seems casual and at ease. There is a second persona whom she adopts for her interviewer, and this second persona is someone who simply takes with greed. She is a confident successful woman, as opposed to the earlier Bohemian version: 'I blossom with arrival, I radiate and I'm ravishing and will change with no one.'

In a third interview she tries to think seriously but ends up putting questions about why she writes. She finally concludes that what she really wants to be is a poet.

These are all plays about women surviving alone, with a transparent honesty about them characteristic of Wesker's work. He is not afraid to allow his characters to talk about emotions, using women to demonstrate independence and thoughtful self-questioning.

Independence in a colonial or post-colonial setting is clearly important to other writers. Brian Friel, a Catholic from Northern Ireland, co-founded a theatre company called Field Day, together with actor Stephen Rea and poets Seamus

Heaney and Tom Paulin, 'to put on plays outside the confines of established theatre, and through that to begin to effect changes in the apathetic atmosphere of the North.'

Translations (1980) previewed in Derry, before transferring to London, is set in 1833 in a hedge-school (an informal, unofficial school run secretly by Catholics) in an Irish-speaking community in County Donegal. In a disused barn Hugh has run reading classes for 35 years. He is a classics scholar whose learning is respected by the village people, including Jimmy, a bachelor in his sixties, fluent in Latin and Greek, and a woman called Sarah, who had a bad speech defect. Maire urges Manus, Hugh's son, to apply for the headship at a new school. He is loath to do so because he thinks his father will apply.

Although the play is in English, it is actually meant to be in Gaelic, a kind of verbal *trompe-l'œil* device. None of the people we see speaks English, although some of them are fluent in Latin. British soldiers are making a new map of the area, and they are introduced by Owen, Hugh's second son. He has made it to Dublin, has servants and property, and he is to act as interpreter for the English soldiers, a go-between between cultures, classes and eras. Captain Lancey speaks a very formal bureaucratic language, translated by Owen into common sense:

> *Lancey*:   This enormous task has been embarked on so that the military authorities will be equipped with up-to-date accurate information on every corner of this part of the Empire.
>
> *Owen*:   The job is being done by soldiers because they are skilled in this work.

At the beginning of Act II, Lieutenant Yolland and Owen go over the Gaelic names, 'every hill, stream, rock, even every patch of ground which possesses its own distinctive Irish name', anglicizing them. Yolland has his reservations about the process which he has been commissioned to undertake as an agency of colonialism. He has a liberal reluctance about him and he says when he arrived in the village: 'I had a curious sensation, it's difficult to describe, it was a momentary sense of discovery; no – not quite a sense of discovery – a recognition or confirmation of something I half knew instinctively. . .' Owen accuses him of being a romantic. Hugh refuses to speak English to Yolland, stating that the Irish language '. . .is a rich language. . .full of the mythologies of fantasy and hope and self-deception, a syntax opulent with tomorrows. It is our response to mud cabins and a diet of potatoes, our only method of replying to. . .inevitabilities'. Owen argues that the language is as outmoded as a place named in memory of some man who has no associations for the people who now live there.

Maire and Yolland dance together. They have no shared language but find a language of love, by reeling off a list of Irish place names.

Yolland has disappeared, leaving total chaos behind him. Lancey threatens that if he is not found all the animals in the village will be killed and then the houses destroyed. The play is open-ended. Owen goes to try and find the men he thinks may have abducted Yolland. Hugh makes reference to the Greek legend about Juno and a new race which will emerge in order to overthrow tyranny.

Before a familiar backdrop about the colonization of Irish culture by the English, Friel creates the dynamic of a self-contained society with its own contradictions. There is attraction between Maire and Yolland and comradeship between Owen and Yolland. Friel also creates a society which cannot sustain itself any longer. Owen has already left, Manus is torn between the desire to establish himself in security and possible marriage and his loyalty to his father.

Aristocrats (1979) is set in a large and decaying house. An outsider, Tom, an American academic, is researching the personal, political and cultural mores of the Roman Catholic aristocracy in Ireland. Judith, the eldest spinster daughter, looks after the old father, who is incontinent and senile. Claire, a daughter in her twenties, is a brilliant pianist, but nervous and on tranquillizers, and is just about to be married. Casimir, another son, has gone to live in Germany and holds on to myths and stories about the family, boasting of its association with almost every famous Irish cultural figure in living memory, including Gerard Manley Hopkins, and James Joyce.

Act II takes place after the family has had lunch together. At the very beginning of the play Willie, a local handyman, fixes a baby alarm so that the father can be heard by Judith anywhere in the house; every so often the dialogue between Judith and Father cuts across the conversation that everybody else is having.

By the end of the play, the family is disintegrating but still held together by memories and its rituals. After her father's death, Judith resolves to take her eight-year-old illegitimate child out of the orphanage in which he has grown up. This culture too has reached a point of no return. It is at a crisis point documented gently and personally with Chekhovian reverberations, but far more dynamic than Chekhov.

Similar explorations of colonial and post-colonial experience can be found in the work of Caribbean playwrights. *Play Mas* (1974) by Mustapha Matura begins in a tailor's shop run by Indians in Trinidad. The characters are preparing for Carnival, talking of independence. Samuel, a Trinidadian, who works for them, comes back wearing a US Marine combat outfit. He at first frightens the Gookool family who own the tailor's shop, but turns out to be only pretending. Samuel then says the Trinidadians have invented the masque that is played at carnivals – the 'Play Mas' of the title – a form of pretence.

After independence Samuel becomes chief of police. Trinidad is in a state of emergency. Samuel is puffed up with pleasure of his new post, and Carnival is coming round again. Ramjohn Gookool brings a message from the people asking Samuel to lift the state of emergency so that Carnival can go ahead. Samuel agrees, but is still worried about people acquiring guns. In the course of Carnival, as Samuel's wife dances with an American, Samuel is himself dressed as a South American general. Under cover of the carnival, gunfire is heard, and an incipient rebellion is put down.

The atmosphere in Matura's plays combines the hard-edged realities of people flexing their political muscle for the first time, with something that feels like a homely township community, with families squabbling over day-to-day trivia. The play points up both innocence and corruptibility, producing a lightly moralistic warning, without really exploring the nature of colonial power.

Matura's *The Coup* was the first play by a black writer to be produced on one of the main stages of the Royal National Theatre (in July 1991). The play opens with a hilariously moving monologue from the Archbishop of Trinidad at the funeral of the leader who gave the island independence. His speech mixes religious prayer and West Indian patois. At the end, he lights a joint.

Mustapha Matura

We flash to a military coup; the president has been imprisoned on charges of corruption. The play is a light but telling and sharp-edged satire, which hints at chaotic political insecurity where danger lurks just beneath the surface. Matura's potent mix of Caribbean patois with the formal language of mother-country bureaucracy is deliberate: In his words 'We in the Caribbean speak in a thinking language, we have retained a manner of speaking where language still has ambiguity, a many-layeredness that the English have lost.'

Mustapha Matura's career as a playwright has also encompassed an involvement with the early stages of so-called 'ethnic' drama. Together with director Charlie Hanson, he founded the Black Theatre Co-operative in 1979; this was one of a number of self-generated ventures designed to raise the profile of West Indian experience; other ventures included a series of 'Black Theatre Seasons' organized from 1983, and the Asian-based Tara Arts, whose director Jatinder Verma applied his and his company's skills to energetic productions of European classics such as Gogol's *Government Inspector* and Moliere's *Tartuffe*. At the end of 1990 a similar project was set up by a group calling themselves the British Chinese Theatre Company, to stage classical Chinese texts using oriental British performers.

8

Back to the drawing room?: Ayckbourn and conclusions

Sir Peter Hall has commented on playwright Alan Ayckbourn: 'If people want to know about life in England in the 60s, 70s and 80s, they will need to study his plays.'

Alan Ayckbourn has been artistic director of various theatres in Scarborough (a seaside resort town in North-East England) for over two decades. Over twenty of his plays have been produced either in London's West End or at the National Theatre, after first being staged in Scarborough. They have been translated into 24 languages and performed on virtually every continent, receiving national and international awards.

Ayckbourn's trilogy of plays, *The Norman Conquests*, produced between 1973 and 1974, is a good example of the ways in which the formal experiments of the so-called 'fringe' fed back into commercial theatre with a new vigour. In the three plays, the same series of events are seen from different points of view.

The first play, *Table Manners*, is superficially a comedy of middle-class married life. It is set in a Victorian vicarage-type building somewhere in the countryside, where Annie looks after her elderly invalid mother. Her brother and sister-in-law are coming down to look after her mother while she plans to spend a dirty weekend with her brother-in-law Norman. In this hotbed of moral and emotional complexity, Norman describes himself as 'a gigolo trapped in a haystack'. His wife Ruth is a successful female executive, which leaves Norman feeling emasculated. His only comeback is to find power in attracting other women and making them happy – a genuine desire. But he is himself a victim of the paradox: 'For God's sake, this is a family, we should care. If we don't care, brothers, sisters, husbands, wives, if we can't finally join hands, what hope is there for anybody?' The reality is that all the characters are locked into family roles with which they are discontented. The dialogue is full of clever naturalistic observations about who is sitting where and what's proper at the dinner table, as if to conceal the fact that no

Alan Ayckbourn

one really likes anyone else, but is nevertheless bound to the family.

The other two plays, *Living Together* and *Round and Round the Garden*, cover the same events from different perspectives. It is as if shifts in gender roles have undermined the traditions of the middle-class, suburban family, and the result is painful, moving and reflected by the deft experimental shifts in time and point of view which makes Ayckbourn such an accomplished observer and technician.

With the work of Alan Ayckbourn, and its commercial success through the 1980s, the British theatre has described a curious circle. In 1952 a play opened in London, which is still running. Agatha Christie's *The Mousetrap* is the story of a country house whose owners (fallen on somewhat hard times) have converted it to a hotel. The first group arrives, only to be snowed in and confronted by mystery and murder. In the course of the investigations, murky personal and family histories are revealed. The façade of secure, respectable, conventional middle-class life is shown to cover insecurities, violence, and unresolved emotional conflicts.

Ayckbourn's work shifts the class basis of the family to post-war suburban territory; he utilizes the imaginative formal experiments of both post-war British playwrights, and the freer climate generated by the younger fringe to play games with both his subject matter and the expectations of his audience. Like more obviously experimental dramatists he presents us with genuine existential dilemmas about the point of view from which we each see reality, and implicitly poses the question of how we achieve consistency and security of point of view.

Although his work is situated on precisely the territory which post-1956 playwrights tried to challenge – the secure middle-class family in a domestic setting – Ayckbourn provides a personal gloss on issues which they explored from a public, more explicitly social point of view. The 'political' angry young (now not so young) men – of whom the best known are the Davids Hare and Edgar and Howard Brenton – provided the link between public school socialism and the varieties of Marxist thought which influenced left-wing political life in the 1970s. Their plays are 'public' plays in the sense that Brecht (a very influential writer from the 1950s to the 1970s) advocated; their plays present individuals self-consciously engaged in public social concerns as part of the historical process. The fact that by and large these individuals are male is still a reflection of the gender-bias deriving from the imaginative process, the fact that the destinies of the theatrical world are still largely controlled by men.

However, the work of women writers has not engaged with the personal in any simplistic, domestic way. The sense of the stage being an epic arena – an empty space which can become anything at any moment, not necessarily hampered by naturalistic sets (closer to the Elizabethan concept of the stage than to our West End proscenium arch, fourth wall conventions) – has been something which women have taken up. Plays flash backwards and forwards in time, and even while many plays by women writers are variants on the rites-of-passage theme – growing up female – this is itself a significant statement of the validity of women's lives as subject matter for drama.

Overwhelmingly, this epic dynamic, which celebrates the freedom of the stage space, has also meant that the close-up interpersonal confrontations which draw the audience in as emotional individuals have been virtually absent in the writing of both men and women. Great passions – personal or political – have been laid aside in favour of kaleidoscopic presentations of slices of contemporary history, social expectation, and the questioning of gender roles. But then, Britain has not generated the kind of passionate realism which is exemplified in the work of American writers like Arthur Miller and Tennessee Williams. The British playwrights of the 1970s and 1980s seized the intellect and the world of ideas – about what is *socially* significant about experience – as their subject matter; they have taken on a self-conscious historical responsibility, whether they define themselves as 'political' or not, because of the political climate in which the richness and variety of post-1968 theatre developed. Of course there has been dross and mediocrity too – but no art can thrive without a variety of achievement.

Despite, therefore, the concerns voiced in public debates about the very survival of the theatre in the 1990s, we still have a theatre landscape second to none: venues range from the amphitheatrical mass of the Royal Shakespeare Theatre's home in London's Barbican Centre to the regional studio theatres redolent of 1960s modernism, to the dimly lit rooms with worn velour chairs in London's pub theatres. Companies vary from the permanent ensembles of the National Theatre, to the jobbing casts of small theatres committed to new writing, to ad hoc and long-term touring companies whose set has to fit into a van, and whose venues may be a proper theatre with a decent lighting rig one night, and a bare school hall the next.

The voices of playwrights range from the brittle elegance of Oxbridge wit to West Indian patois, to the minimalism of experimentalists, and include the experiences of women and of sexual and ethnic minorities. Debate continues to rage about the nature of gender bias in the theatre – can men only write well about men? Can women only write well about women? Is there such a thing as 'ghetto' writing? Performers discuss the different ways in which the increasing presence of actors and actresses of different ethnic origins make their singular contributions to theatre: Should they generate their own companies, or should they aim to integrate fully into the existing system? Small touring companies continue to work in a variety of ways: some commissioning writers and hiring directors, some researching, devising and writing their own work more collectively. Whatever points of view we may have on any of these questions, they could not have been so variously and vigorously expressed in British theatre at any time before 1970.

Select Bibliography

This section of the bibliography only includes first editions of works produced by the authors since 1970.

ARDEN, **John**

Two Autobiographical Plays: The True History of Squire Jonathan and his Unfortunate Treasure and *The Bagman or the Impromptu of Muswell Hill* (1971)
The Island of the Mighty (with Margaretta D'Arcy) (1978)

AYCKBOURN, **Alan**

Mixed Doubles (1970)
How the Other Half Loves (1972)
Time and Time Again (1973)
Absurd Person Singular (1974)
The Norman Conquests: Table Manners, Living Together and Round and Round the Garden (1974)
Absent Friends (1975)
Three Plays (Absurd Person Singular, Bedroom Farce and Absent Friends) (1977)
Confusions (1977)
Ten Times Table (1978)
Joking Apart and Other Plays (1979)
Sisterly Feelings and Taking Steps (1981)
A Chorus of Disapproval (1986)
Woman in Mind (1986)
A Small Family Business (1988)
Man of the Moment (1990)

BOND, **Edward**

The Pope's Wedding and Other Plays (1971)
Lear (1972)

The Sea (1973)
Bingo (1974)
The Fool and We Come to The River (1976)
Stone and A-A-America (1976)
The Bundle (1978)
The Woman (1979)
The War Plays (1983)

BRENTON, **Howard**

Revenge, (1970)
Christie in Love and Other Plays (1970)
Plays For Public Places (1972)
Magnificence (1974)
The Churchill Play (1974)
Weapons of Happiness (1976)
The Saliva Milkshake (1977)
Epsom Downs (1977)
Sore Throats and Sonnets of Love and Opposition (1979)
The Romans in Britain (1982)
Thirteenth Night and (with **Tony Howard***) A Short Sharp Shock* (1981)
The Genius (1983)
Bloody Poetry (1985)
Dead Head (1987)
H.I.D. (Hess Is Dead) (1989)

CHURCHILL, **Caryl**

Owners (1973)
Light Shining in Buckinghamshire (1977)
Traps (1978)

Cloud Nine (1979)
Top Girls (1984)
Fen and Softcops (1986)
Serious Money (1987)

CLARK, Brian

Whose Life Is It Anyway? (1978)
Can You Hear Me at the Back?
(1979)
The Petition (1986)

EDGAR, David

Dick Deterred (1974)
Destiny (1976)
Wreckers (1977)
Ball Boys (1978)
The Jail Diary of Albie Sachs (1978)
Mary Barnes (1979)
Teendreams (1979)
Maydays (1984)
That Summer (1987)
Entertaining Strangers (1988)
Shorts (1990)

FRIEL, Brian

Translations (1980)
Aristocracy (1979)

GEMS, Pam

Dusa, Fish, Stas and Vi (1978)
Piaf (1979)
Three Plays (Piaf, Camille and Loving Women) (1985)

GREIG, Noel

The Dear Love of Comrades (1989)

GRIFFITHS, Trevor

Occupations and The Big House
(1972)
The Party (1974)
Comedians (1976)
Through the Night (1977)
Such Impossibilities (1977)
Apricots and Thermidor (1978)
Country: A Tory Story (1981)
Oi for England (1982)
Real Dreams (1987)

HARE, David

Slag (1971)
The Great Exhibition (1972)
Knuckle (1974)
Wetherby (1975)
Fanshen (1976)
Teeth 'n' Smiles (1976)
Plenty (1978)
Licking Hitler (1978)
Plenty (1978)
Dreams of Leaving (1980)
The Asian Plays (Fanshen, Saigon and A Map of the World) (1986)
The Bay at Nice and Wrecked Eggs
(1986)
Racing Demon (1989)

McDONALD, Sharman

When I Was a Girl I Used to Scream and Shout (1984)

McGRATH, John

Random Happenings in the Hebrides
(1972)
The Cheviot, the Stag and the Black, Black, Black Oil (1973)

MUSTAPHA, Matura

Play Mas (1974)
The Coup (1991)

Index